Gretchen Bitterlin
Dennis Johnson
Donna Price
Sylvia Ramirez
K. Lynn Savage

Ventures Transitions

STUDENT'S BOOK

CAMBRIDGE
UNIVERSITY PRESS

CAMBRIDGE UNIVERSITY PRESS
Cambridge, New York, Melbourne, Madrid, Cape Town, Singapore, São Paulo,
Delhi, Mexico City

Cambridge University Press
32 Avenue of the Americas, New York, NY 10013-2473, USA

www.cambridge.org
Information on this title: www. cambridge.org/9780521186131

First published 2010

Printed in the United States of America

A catalog record for this publication is available from the British Library

ISBN 978-0-521-18613-1 Student's Book and Audio CD
ISBN 978-0-521-18614-8 Workbook
ISBN 978-0-521-18615-5 Teacher's Manual

Cambridge University Press has no responsibility for the persistence or
accuracy of URLs for external or third-party Internet Web sites referred to in
this publication, and does not guarantee that any content on such Web sites is,
or will remain, accurate or appropriate.

Book design: Adventure House, NYC
Layout services: Page Designs International
Photo research: Pronk & Associates, Inc.
Audio production: Richard LePage and Associates

To the teacher

What is *Transitions*?

Transitions offers standards-based, integrated-skills material to help prepare adult students for success at work or in an academic setting. Aimed at low-advanced students, *Transitions* focuses on developing reading and writing skills and features high-interest topics such as building self-confidence, managing interviews, and having a positive attitude.

Unit organization

Within each unit there are five lessons:

LESSON A Get ready The opening lesson focuses students on the topic of the unit. The initial exercise, *Talk about the pictures*, creates student interest and activates students' prior knowledge about the topic. The visuals help the teacher assess what learners already know and serve as a prompt for the key vocabulary of each unit. Next is *Listening*, which is based on a mini-lecture. A note-taking exercise helps students practice listening for main ideas and important details. The lesson concludes with a communicative activity that gives students an opportunity to practice language related to the theme.

LESSON B focuses on practical grammar. The sections move from a *Grammar focus* that presents the grammar point in chart form; to *Practice* exercises that check comprehension of the grammar point and provide guided practice; and, finally, to *Communicate* exercises that guide learners as they generate original answers and conversations.

LESSONS C and **D Reading** develop reading skills and expand vocabulary. The lesson opens with a *Before you read* exercise whose purpose is to activate prior knowledge and encourage learners to make predictions. Next, in *Read*, students read a passage of several paragraphs on a high-interest topic related to the theme of the unit. The reading is followed by *After you read* exercises that check students' understanding and use the reading as a springboard for vocabulary building. The lesson concludes with an activity for practicing summarizing skills.

LESSON E Writing provides writing practice within the context of the unit. This lesson has three sections: *Before you write*, *Write*, and *After you write*. The exercises in *Before you write* provide warm-up activities to activate the language students will need for the writing task, followed by a writing model and exercises to help students plan the writing they will do in the next section. The *Write* section provides the writing prompt and refers to previous exercises to help guide students' writing. *After you write* provides opportunities for students to check their own work and to share and react to a classmate's writing.

What components does *Transitions* have?

Student's Book with Audio CD

Each **Student's Book** contains ten topic-focused units. Each unit has five skill-focused lessons. The audio CD contains recordings of all lectures.

Workbook

The Workbook is a natural extension of the Student's Book. It has one page of exercises for each lesson in the Student's Book. Workbook exercises can be assigned in class, for homework, or as student support when a class is missed. Students can check their own answers with the answer key in the back of the Workbook. If used in class, the Workbook can extend classroom instructional time by 35 to 40 minutes per lesson.

Teacher's Manual

The Teacher's Manual provides generic lesson plan guidelines for each lesson in a unit as well as lesson-specific notes. The notes include warm-up activities for all the note-taking exercises and suggestions on how to expand certain other exercises. The Student's Book answer key and the audio script for the Lesson A listening exercises are provided at the back of the Teacher's Manual.

MP3 files for the reading passages

The reading passages in the Student's Book are provided as MP3 files, which can be downloaded from www.cambridge.org/transitions.

The Author Team

Gretchen Bitterlin   Sylvia Ramirez
Dennis Johnson   K. Lynn Savage
Donna Price

Scope and sequence

UNIT TITLE / TOPIC	LISTENING AND SPEAKING	VOCABULARY
Unit 1 **Selling yourself** pages 2–11 **Topic:** Job skills	• "Hard" and "soft" skills • Talking about job skills	• Language for talking about goals • Job skills • Personal qualities
Unit 2 **Building self-confidence** pages 12–21 **Topic:** Self-confidence	• Comparing workers' strengths and weaknesses • Defining and discussing self-confidence	• Self-confidence terms • Personal strength adjectives
Unit 3 **Volunteering** pages 22–31 **Topic:** Volunteer work	• Volunteering • Discussing reasons for volunteering • Discussing volunteer opportunities	• Prefixes • Gerunds • Nouns for the doer of an action
Unit 4 **Effective job applications** pages 32–41 **Topic:** Job search	• Steps in the job search process • Talking about applying for a job	• Suffixes • Phrasal verbs
Unit 5 **Successful interviews** pages 42–51 **Topic:** Job interviews	• Rules for making a good first impression • Talking about first impressions • Talking about mistakes you've made	• Guessing meaning from context • Understanding idioms

GRAMMAR FOCUS	READING	WRITING
• Participial adjectives	• Setting goals for the future • Keys for success at work	• Creating a resume
• The present passive	• Understanding self-confidence • Building self-confidence	• Writing a paragraph that identifies a strength and provides supporting examples
• Indirect (reported) statements	• Family volunteering • Volunteering while at college	• Clustering • Writing a summary paragraph about an article
• Past perfect	• Reading about online scams • Tips for filling out job applications	• Writing a cover letter
• Past modals: *Should(n't) have, could have*	• Keys for a successful interview • Following up after an interview	• Writing a thank-you note

UNIT TITLE TOPIC	LISTENING AND SPEAKING	VOCABULARY
Unit 6 **Small talk** **pages 52–61** **Topic:** Making small talk	• Purposes of small talk • Appropriate and inappropriate small-talk topics	• Verb + preposition + -*ing* combinations • Phrasal verbs
Unit 7 **Improving relationships** **pages 62–71** **Topic:** Teamwork	• The importance and benefits of teamwork • Discussing teamwork • Giving advice about problems in the workplace	• Punctuation, phrases, and clauses to signal definitions • Understanding idioms
Unit 8 **Giving and receiving criticism** **pages 72–81** **Topic:** Types of criticism	• Negative and constructive criticism • Discussing experiences with criticism • Discussing regrets	• Adverbs ending in -*ly* • Defining slang expressions
Unit 9 **The right attitude** **pages 82–91** **Topic:** Positive and negative attitudes	• Behaviors of positive and negative people • Discussing positive and negative attitudes	• Positive and negative words and phrases • Suffixes for different parts of speech
Unit 10 **Writing at work and school** **pages 92–101** **Topic:** Writing	• The importance of writing • Talking about things people write at work and school	• Synonyms and antonyms • Multiple meanings of words

GRAMMAR FOCUS	READING	WRITING
• Tag questions	• Small talk, big problems • Strategies for successful small talk	• Writing a paragraph comparing appropriate and inappropriate topics for small talk
• The present unreal conditional	• Bad behavior in the workplace • Approaches to dealing with annoying people in the workplace	• Writing a letter giving advice about a problem at work or at school
• Past unreal conditional	• Accepting criticism gracefully • The performance evaluation	• Writing a story about a time when someone criticized you
• Adverb clauses of concession: *although* and *even though*	• The power of positive thinking • Avoiding a negative attitude	• Writing a college admissions essay
• Causative verbs: *make*, *have*, and *get*	• E-mail etiquette • Good business writing	• Writing an action plan

Correlations

UNIT/PAGES	CASAS	EFF
Unit 1 **Selling yourself** Pages 2–11	0.1.2, 0.1.5, 0.1.6, 0.2.1, 0.2.4, 2.3.1, 2.3.2, 2.5.5, 2.7.6, 4.1.4, 4.1.7, 4.1.8, 4.1.9, 4.4.1, 4.4.2, 4.6.1, 4.8.1, 4.8.2, 4.8.3, 4.9.1, 6.0.1, 7.1.1, 7.1.4, 7.2.1, 7.2.2, 7.4.1, 7.4.2, 7.4.5, 7.5.1	Most EFF standards are met, with particular focus on: • Conveying ideas in writing • Speaking so others can understand • Taking responsibility for learning • Listening actively • Cooperating with others
Unit 2 **Building self-confidence** Pages 12–21	0.1.1, 0.1.4, 0.1.6, 0.2.1, 0.2.4, 2.5.1, 2.8.2, 3.1.2, 3.1.3, 3.5.9, 3.6.4, 3.6.5, 4.1.1, 4.1.2, 4.4.1, 4.6.1, 4.8.1, 4.8.5, 4.8.7, 7.1.1, 7.1.4, 8.3.1	Most EFF standards are met, with particular focus on: • Speaking so others can understand • Listening actively • Cooperating with others • Guiding others • Advocating and influencing • Resolving conflict and negotiating
Unit 3 **Volunteering** Pages 22–31	0.1.1, 0.1.4, 0.1.7, 0.2.1, 1.9.1, 2.2.1, 2.5.1, 2.7.2, 2.7.3, 2.8.3, 2.8.9, 4.3.2, 4.6.1, 4.6.4, 4.8.1, 4.8.2, 7.3.1, 7.3.2, 7.3.3	Most EFF standards are met, with particular focus on: • Speaking so others can understand • Cooperating with others • Guiding others • Solving problems and making decisions • Planning
Unit 4 **Effective job applications** Pages 32–41	0.1.4, 0.2.1, 0.2.4, 1.9.1, 2.1.1, 2.2.1, 2.3.1, 4.1.1, 4.1.2, 4.1.3, 4.1.4, 4.1.5, 4.1.6, 4.1.7, 4.1.8, 4.2.1, 4.2.3, 4.4.1, 4.4.7	Most EFF standards are met, with particular focus on: • Reading with understanding • Conveying ideas in writing • Speaking so others can understand • Listening actively • Cooperating with others
Unit 5 **Successful interviews** Pages 42–51	0.1.1, 0.1.2, 0.1.3, 0.1.4, 0.2.1, 0.2.2, 0.2.3, 2.3.1, 4.1.1, 4.1.2, 4.1.5, 4.1.6, 4.1.7, 4.1.8, 4.1.9, 4.2.1, 4.2.5, 4.4.1, 4.4.4, 4.4.5, 4.5.1, 4.5.2, 4.5.4, 4.8.1, 6.0.1, 7.1.3, 7.2.1	Most EFF standards are met, with particular focus on: • Speaking so others can understand • Listening actively • Cooperating with others • Taking responsibility for learning

SCANS	BEST Plus Form A	BEST Form B
Most SCANS standards are met, with particular focus on: • Acquiring and evaluating information • Participating as a member of a team • Teaching others new skills • Understanding systems	Overall test preparation is supported, with particular impact on the following items: • Locator: W1, W2, W3, W4, W5 • Level 1: 1.1, 2.1, 2.2, 2.3, 4.2 • Level 2: 1.2, 2.1, 3.2, 3.3 • Level 3: 1.2, 1.3, 2.1, 2.2, 2.3	Overall test preparation is supported, with particular impact on the following areas: • Oral interview • Personal information / identification • Reading passages • Writing notes • Time / Numbers • Reading signs, ads, and notices • Employment / Training
Most SCANS standards are met, with particular focus on: • Participating as a member of a team • Teaching others new skills • Working with diversity • Negotiating • Understanding systems	Overall test preparation is supported, with particular impact on the following items: • W3, W5-6 • Level 1: 3.3, 4.2 • Level 2: 2.3 • Level 3: 4.2	Overall test preparation is supported, with particular impact on the following areas: • Oral interview • Personal information • Communication • Directions / Clarification • Employment / Training
Most SCANS standards are met, with particular focus on: • Participating as a member of a team • Teaching others new skills • Exercising leadership • Working with diversity • Acquiring and using information • Understanding systems	Overall test preparation is supported, with particular impact on the following items: • Level 1: 3.2, 3.3, 4.2 • Level 2: 2.2, 2.3 • Level 3: 2.2, 4.2	Overall test preparation is supported, with particular impact on the following areas: • Oral interview • Personal information • Communication • Directions / Clarification • Listening comprehension • Reading • Writing
Most SCANS standards are met, with particular focus on: • Human resources • Serving customers • Exercising leadership • Negotiating • Working with diversity • Acquiring and using information • Understanding complex inter-relationships	Overall test preparation is supported, with particular impact on the following items: • W1, W2, • Level 1: 3.2, 4.2 • Level 2: 1.2, 1.3, 5.2 • Level 3: 3.1	Overall test preparation is supported, with particular impact on the following areas: • Reading • Writing • Fluency • Communication • Personal information • Time / Numbers
Most SCANS standards are met, with particular focus on: • Participating as a member of a team • Exercising leadership • Acquiring and using information • Understanding complex inter-relationships	Overall test preparation is supported, with particular impact on the following items: • W1, W2, • Level 1: 3.2, 4.2 • Level 2: 1.2, 1.3, 5.2 • Level 3: 3.1	Overall test preparation is supported, with particular impact on the following areas: • Reading • Writing • Fluency • Communication • Personal information • Time / Numbers

UNIT/PAGES	CASAS	EFF
Unit 6 **Small talk** Pages 52–61	0.1.1, 0.1.2, 0.1.4, 0.1.6, 0.1.8, 0.2.1, 0.2.4, 2.2.1, 2.3.3, 2.6.1, 2.7.1, 2.7.2	Most EFF standards are met, with particular focus on: • Speaking so others can understand • Listening actively • Cooperating with others
Unit 7 **Improving relationships** Pages 62–71	0.1.1, 0.1.2, 0.1.3, 0.1.4, 0.1.6, 0.2.1, 1.2.1, 1.2.6, 1.3.1, 1.4.1, 1.6.1, 2.1.7, 2.2.1, 2.6.3, 2.7.6, 2.7.7, 2.7.8, 2.7.9, 2.8.3, 2.8.4, 2.8.6, 4.2.1, 4.3.2, 4.4.1, 4.4.3, 4.4.4, 4.6.1, 4.6.2, 4.6.4, 4.8.1, 4.8.2, 4.8.5, 4.8.6, 7.3.1, 7.3.2, 7.3.3	Most EFF standards are met, with particular focus on: • Speaking so others can understand • Listening actively • Cooperating with others • Solving problems and making decisions
Unit 8 **Giving and receiving criticism** Pages 72–81	0.1.1, 0.1.2, 0.1.3, 0.1.6, 0.1.7, 0.1.8, 4.4.1, 4.4.2, 4.4.4, 4.6.1, 4.8.1, 4.8.2, 4.8.5, 4.8.6	Most EFF standards are met, with particular focus on: • Listening actively • Cooperating with others • Reflecting and evaluating
Unit 9 **The right attitude** Pages 82–91	0.1.1, 0.1.2, 0.1.3, 0.1.6, 0.1.7, 0.1.8, 0.2.1, 4.4.1, 4.4.2, 4.4.4, 4.4.7, 4.6.1, 4.6.5, 4.8.1, 4.8.3, 4.8.5, 4.8.6, 4.8.7	Most EFF standards are met, with particular focus on: • Listening actively • Cooperating with others • Guiding others • Advocating and influencing • Resolving conflict and negotiating • Solving problems and making decisions
Unit 10 **Writing at work and school** Pages 92–101	0.2.2, 0.2.3, 1.7.6, 2.3.4, 2.4.1, 3.2.1, 4.4.7, 4.5.2, 4.5.5, 4.6.2, 4.6.5, 4.7.1, 4.7.4, 5.4.1, 7.1.4, 7.4.2, 7.7.2, 7.7.4	Most EFF standards are met, with particular focus on: • Conveying ideas in writing • Solving problems and making decisions • Taking responsibility for learning • Learning through research • Reflecting and evaluating • Using information and communications technology

SCANS	BEST Plus Form A	BEST Form B
Most SCANS standards are met, with particular focus on: • Acquiring and using information • Understanding complex inter-relationships	Overall test preparation is supported, with particular impact on the following items: • W1, W2, W3, W5 • W6, W7, W8 • Level 1: 1.2, 3.2 • Level 2: 1.2, 3.1 • Level 3: 1.1, 3.1	Overall test preparation is supported, with particular impact on the following areas: • Fluency • Communication • Personal information
Most SCANS standards are met, with particular focus on: • Participating as a member of a team • Exercising leadership • Acquiring and using information • Monitoring and correcting performance	Overall test preparation is supported, with particular impact on the following items: • W1, W2, W3, W4 • Level 1: 2.1, 2.3 • Level 2: 2.1, 2.3 • Level 3: 1.2, 3.3, 4.1	Overall test preparation is supported, with particular impact on the following areas: • Fluency • Communication • Personal information • Directions / Clarification • Listening comprehension
Most SCANS standards are met, with particular focus on: • Participating as a member of a team • Exercising leadership • Acquiring and evaluating information	Overall test preparation is supported, with particular impact on the following items: • Level 1: 2.3 • Level 2: 2.3, 3.2 • Level 3: 1.3, 2.1, 2.2	Overall test preparation is supported, with particular impact on the following areas: • Fluency • Communication • Personal information • Listening comprehension
Most SCANS standards are met, with particular focus on: • Participating as a member of a team • Exercising leadership • Negotiating • Working with diversity • Acquiring and evaluating information	Overall test preparation is supported, with particular impact on the following items: • W4, W7, W8 • Level 1: 2.2, 2.3, 4.2, 4.3 • Level 2: 1.3, 2.1, 2.2, 3.2, 3.3 • Level 3: 1.2, 1.3, 2.1, 2.2, 2.3, 3.3, 4.2	Overall test preparation is supported, with particular impact on the following areas: • Fluency • Communication • Personal information • Listening comprehension
Most SCANS standards are met, with particular focus on: • Acquiring and evaluating information • Organizing and maintaining information • Interpreting and communicating information • Using computers to process information • Understanding systems • Monitoring and correcting performance • Working with a variety of technologies	Overall test preparation is supported, with particular impact on the following items: • W6, W7, W8 • Level 1: 2.3, 4.2, 4.3 • Level 2: 2.3, 3.2, 3.3, 4.2 • Level 3: 1.2, 1.3, 2.1, 2.2, 2.3, 3.2, 3.3, 4.2, 5.1, 5.2	Overall test preparation is supported, with particular impact on the following areas: • Writing notes • Reading • Writing • Fluency • Communication

Get ready

Selling yourself

1 Talk about the pictures

A What kinds of skills do people need in order to find a good job these days?

B Describe the people in the photos. What skills do you think they have? Do you have these skills?

2 Listening

A 🔘 **Listen** and answer the questions.

1. What are two types of job skills?
2. Which type is more important?

B 🔘 **Listen again.** Take notes on the key information.

Topic: Two types of job skills

A.

   1. Definition:

   2. Examples:

B.

   1. Definition:

   2. Examples:

Conclusion

Listen again. Check your notes. Did you miss anything important?

C **Exchange** notes with a partner. Do the notes answer these questions?

1. What are hard skills?
2. What are soft skills?
3. Which type of skill is more important?

D **Discuss.** Talk with your classmates.

1. What kind of job do you want to have in the future?
2. Which hard and soft skills will you need?
3. What do you plan to do in order to get the skills you need?

Participipial adjectives

1 Grammar focus: Adjectives ending in *-ed* and *-ing*

Adjective *-ed*	Adjective *-ing*	
I'm interested in this job.	This is an interesting job.	This job is interesting.
He's excited to do the work.	This is exciting work.	The work is exciting.

Verb forms that end in *-ed* or *-ing* are called *participles*. There is a difference in meaning between the *-ed* and the *-ing* forms. Often, the *-ed* form describes the way someone feels, and the *-ing* form describes a situation, thing, or person.

2 Practice

A Write. Circle the correct adjective.

1. **A** Josie, how did your job interview at the library go last week?

   B It was really (tiring) / tired.

2. **A** Why?

   B It was pretty long. But it was also **excited** / **exciting**.

3. **A** What did they ask you?

   B They asked if I was **interested** / **interesting** in books.

4. **A** Did they ask you anything else?

   B They wanted to know if it was **motivated** / **motivating** for me to work on a team or if I preferred working alone.

5. **A** Do you think you'll get the job?

   B They asked me to come for a second interview tomorrow. I'm so **thrilled** / **thrilling**!

6. **A** I have an interview at the hospital tomorrow. Do you have any advice for me?

   B Show the employer how **dedicated** / **dedicating** you are.

7. **A** Anything else?

   B If you don't get the job, don't be **frustrated** / **frustrating**.

8. **A** Well, I would be **disappointed** / **disappointing**.

   B Just think of it as good interviewing experience.

B Talk with a partner. Take turns asking and answering the questions. Choose a participial adjective from the list in your answers.

amazed / amazing	embarrassed / embarrassing	bored / boring
amused / amusing	frightened / frightening	excited / exciting
surprised / surprising	disappointed / disappointing	annoyed / annoying

How do teachers feel when their students are late?

They feel annoyed.

1. How do teachers feel when their students are late?
2. How did Sarah feel when she didn't get her dream job?
3. How does it feel when someone criticizes you in front of other people?
4. What was your opinion about the last movie you saw?
5. What is your opinion about dangerous sports like rock climbing or motorcycle racing?
6. In his job, David sees the same people and does exactly the same things every day. What kind of job does he have?

Write sentences about the situations. Use participial adjectives.

Teachers feel annoyed when their students are late.

3 Communicate

A Work in a small group. Take turns asking and answering questions about your experiences. Use the adjectives from Exercise 2B.

What's a frustrating experience you've had at school or work?

I was frustrated when I got a low score on a test after I studied for five hours.

1. What is the most exciting thing that has happened to you recently?
2. Have you ever been depressed?
3. What is an amusing movie or TV show you've seen recently?
4. Is there anything about life in the United States that is surprising for you?
5. [your own question]

B Share information with your classmates.

1 Before you read

Talk with your classmates. Answer the questions.

1. What are your goals for the next one, two, or three years?
2. Why are some goals easier than others? Why are some more difficult?

2 Read

Read the article.

To listen to a recording of the reading,
go to www.cambridge.org/transitions

Setting Goals for the Future

What do you want your future to look like? Do you want to develop skills for a better job? Do you want to graduate from college? No matter what you want in the future, one of the best ways to get there is by setting goals.

Setting a goal means making a decision about what you want to achieve. It requires finding out what you need to do to achieve that goal and planning how long it will take you to do it.

Making choices about the future can be difficult because we often focus only on the present. In order to think about your future goals, take a few minutes and imagine what you want your life to be like in one, two, or three years. Where will you be? What will you be doing? How will you feel?

There are a number of important points for you to keep in mind when setting a goal. It should be detailed, measurable, and realistic, and it should have a completion date.

Once you have a goal in mind, try to add as much detail as possible. Adding detail will make the goal clearer. For example, instead of saying "I want to get a better job," you can add details, such as "I want to study cooking so that I can be a chef." Details like "study cooking" and "be a chef" clearly show what you want to achieve and how you plan to achieve it.

In addition to adding detail to your goal, make sure you can measure your progress. "I want a better education" is a good goal, but it is difficult to measure. How will you know when your goal is completed? "I will apply to three colleges next spring" is a better goal because you can pay attention to your progress.

Goals should be challenging, but they should not be too difficult. An impossible goal will lead to failure. You can avoid failure by making sure your goal is realistic. Becoming a professional soccer player might be your dream, but is it realistic? Instead, set your goal on something more achievable, like playing for a local team.

Finally, make sure your goal has a completion date, or deadline. If you know when you want to complete your goal, you will be more motivated. Without a deadline, people often stop paying attention to their goal. Just as your goal should be realistic, your deadline should be realistic also.

3 After you read

A Check your understanding.

1. What does *setting a goal* mean? _____

_____

2. The article describes four characteristics of a good goal. What are they? _____

_____

3. Why should a goal be detailed? _____

_____

4. Why shouldn't you have a goal that is too difficult? _____

_____

5. What happens when people have a goal without a deadline? _____

_____

B Build your vocabulary.

1. Underline the words from the chart in the reading. Then use a dictionary and write the correct definition to fit the meaning of the words as they are used in the reading.

Vocabulary	Definition
1. progress (n.)	*movement toward a goal*
2. realistic (adj.)	
3. measure (v.)	
4. challenging (adj.)	
5. achieve (v.)	

2. Use the words in the chart to form sentences about your goals.

C Summarize the reading. Work with a partner and take turns restating the main points. Then work together to write a summary. Include the following:

1. definition of setting a goal
2. four characteristics of a good goal

1 Before you read

Talk with your classmates. Answer the questions.

1. What types of skills do employers look for?
2. What types of personal qualities do employers look for?

2 Read

Read the article.

To listen to a recording of the reading,
go to www.cambridge.org/transitions

Keys for Success at Work

Many people think that employers are only interested in technical skills when they interview new candidates for a job; however, in today's job market, most companies are looking for much more. Different companies have different needs, yet there are a number of general skills and qualities they all hope to find. These skills include:

Communication skills – Companies are interested in people who can communicate and get along well with others. The way you organize your thoughts, express your ideas, and deal positively with customers and co-workers is what will impress employers the most.

Leadership skills – Many companies ask for people who are "self-starters" and who are willing to lead others. In other words, employers want people who can think for themselves and who aren't afraid to make independent decisions.

Maturity – A mature employee is someone who manages time well, takes responsibility for mistakes, and does not become frustrated in challenging situations.

Problem-solving skills – Problem-solving and critical-thinking skills are also very important to employers. Companies value employees who are able to recognize problems, develop a plan for solving them, and follow through with that plan.

Commitment – Employers prefer workers who work hard toward the company's goals. They want to hire team players who are committed to their jobs.

Informational skills – Your ability to gather, organize, and analyze information is very important in today's world. Knowing how to use a computer to search the Internet, send e-mails, and solve problems is key in almost every profession.

As you can see, most of these do not involve technical skills. They are "people skills" that are important in every job or field. If you lack any of these skills or qualities, you should look for ways to develop them as part of your goal setting for the future.

3 After you read

A Interpret the article. Work with a partner. Match each skill with the *best* example. Write the letter of the example in the blank.

Skill

_____ 1. communication

_____ 2. leadership

_____ 3. maturity

_____ 4. problem solving

_____ 5. commitment

_____ 6. informational

Example

a. A new worker at an ice cream store forgets to close the freezer and the ice cream melts. He offers to pay for the ice cream and promises to be more careful in the future.

b. A company needs to find ways to save money. A worker thinks of a plan to save money by reducing the amount of paper that the company is wasting.

c. Melinda's company has an important deadline tomorrow. Her co-workers go home at 5:30 p.m., but she works late into the evening to help the company meet its deadline.

d. A customer at a dry cleaning store is upset because the cleaner damaged his suit. The cashier listens politely and offers to pay for the damage. The customer is satisfied.

e. An auto worker knows how to use a complex computer program to analyze the problem with a customer's car.

f. At a factory, the workers complain that the lunchroom is unattractive. A worker organizes and supervises a group of volunteers who come in on the weekend to decorate the lunchroom.

B Build your vocabulary. Underline the words or phrases from the chart in the reading. Use a dictionary and write the correct definition to fit the reading. Write one or two related words and their part of speech.

Word in reading	Definition	Related words
1. impress (v.)	*to please somebody deeply*	*impression (n.), impressive (adj.)*
2. get along with (v.)		
3. maturity (n.)		
4. committed (adj.)		
5. value (v.)		
6. analyze (v.)		

C Summarize the reading. Work with a partner and take turns restating the main points. Then work together to write a summary. Include the following:

1. communication skills

2. leadership skills

3. maturity

4. problem-solving skills

5. commitment

6. informational skills

1 Before you write

A Talk with a partner. Answer the questions.

1. Why are résumés important for a job?
2. Do you have a résumé? Have you ever used a résumé when you looked for a job?

B Read the sample résumé.

Renee Smith

200 Chestnut Rd., Atlanta, GA 30341
(404) 555-1111 • jsmith@cup.org

OBJECTIVE

Teacher's Assistant in a preschool. I am organized, hardworking, and dedicated to working as a team member. I am very interested in working with children with disabilities.

EDUCATION

AA, Early Childhood Education
Atlanta Metropolitan College, Atlanta, GA

High School Diploma
International High School, Atlanta, GA

EXPERIENCE

Teacher's Aide
Little Angels Preschool, Athens, GA
June 2010–present

Tutor
Center for Autism, Athens, GA
October 2009–June 2010

REFERENCES

Available on request

C Work with a partner. Answer the questions.

1. Whose résumé is this?
2. What job would this person like to have?
3. What adjectives did this person use to describe herself?
4. Where did this person go to college and high school? What degree does she have?
5. What job experience does she have?
6. How can employers get her references?

D Plan your résumé. Complete the information.

1. Your name and address: _____

2. Your job objective (the kind of job you'd like to have): _____

3. Adjectives that describe you as a worker: _____

4. Where you went to school: _____

5. Any job experience that you've had: _____

6. Your references: _____

2 Write

Write your résumé. Use the résumé in Exercise 1B and your outline in Exercise 1D to help you. (Note: You do not need to include references in your résumé, but you must have them if an employer asks for them.)

3 After you write

A Check your writing.

	Yes	No
1. I included my name, address, phone, and e-mail.	☐	☐
2. I included my job objective.	☐	☐
3. I included my education and job experience.	☐	☐
4. I included information about my references.	☐	☐
5. I included adjectives that describe me as a worker.	☐	☐

B Share your writing with a partner.

1. Exchange résumés with your partner. Read your partner's résumé.
2. Comment on your partner's résumé. Ask your partner a question about the résumé. Tell your partner one thing you learned.

Get ready

Building self-confidence

1 Talk about the pictures

A How do you define self-confidence?

B Do you think the people in the photos are self-confident? Why or why not?

2 Listening

A  **Listen** and answer the questions.

1. What was the listening about?
2. Who is more self-confident, David or Sarah? Why?

B **Listen again.** Take notes on the key information.

> David
>
>   Strengths:
>
>
>   Weaknesses:
>
>
>
>
> Sarah
>
>   Strengths:
>
>
>   Weaknesses:

Listen again. Check your answers. Did you miss anything important?

C **Exchange** notes with a partner. Do the notes answer the following questions?

1. What are David's strengths and weaknesses?
2. What are Sarah's strengths and weaknesses?

D **Discuss.** Talk with your classmates.

1. Do you agree with the decision to promote David? Why or why not?
2. Why do you think self-confident people are more successful?
3. Are you self-confident? Why or why not?

The present passive

1 Grammar focus: Subject + *be* + past participle

Passive sentences have the form subject + *be* + past participle. A passive verb is used to focus on what happens to the subject. A phrase consisting of *by* + noun comes after the passive verb only if it is important to know who or what performs the action.

Active	Passive
<u>Life experiences</u> affect self-confidence.	Self-confidence is affected by <u>life experiences.</u>
<u>The support you receive</u> determines your inner feelings.	Your inner feelings are determined by <u>the support you receive.</u>

2 Practice

A Write. Is the sentence active or passive? Write *A* or *P*.

_P_ 1. The employees are encouraged by their supervisor to have a good attitude.

_____ 2. Charles is often criticized by his professors for being late.

_____ 3. The economy discourages Mr. Chung from leaving his job.

_____ 4. Hugo's job performance is improved by being more positive.

_____ 5. Sun Mi is motivated by Kevin's hard work.

_____ 6. Mr. Chu improves his résumé using the Internet.

_____ 7. Carmela criticizes Kevin for being late.

Change the passive sentences to active sentences. Change the active sentences to passive sentences.

8. *The supervisor encourages the employees to have a good attitude.*

9. _____

10. _____

11. _____

12. _____

13. _____

14. _____

B **Talk** with a partner. Read the ad for the self-confidence workshop. Discuss the questions below.

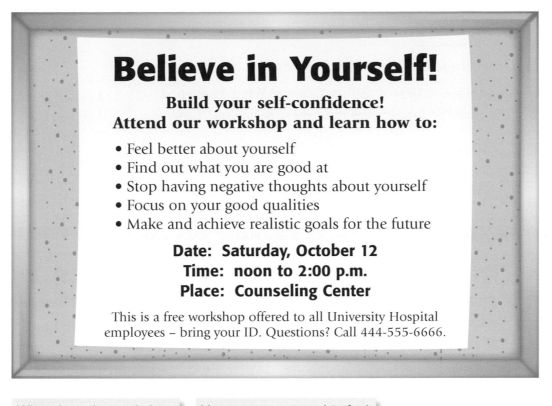

Believe in Yourself!

Build your self-confidence!
Attend our workshop and learn how to:

- Feel better about yourself
- Find out what you are good at
- Stop having negative thoughts about yourself
- Focus on your good qualities
- Make and achieve realistic goals for the future

Date: Saturday, October 12
Time: noon to 2:00 p.m.
Place: Counseling Center

This is a free workshop offered to all University Hospital employees – bring your ID. Questions? Call 444-555-6666.

> What does the workshop encourage you to do?

> You are encouraged to feel better about yourself.

1. What does it discourage you from doing?
2. Where is the workshop located?
3. To whom is the workshop offered?
4. When is the workshop scheduled?

Write answers to the questions. Use the present passive.

3 Communicate

A **Work** with a partner. Talk about self-confidence. Use these phrases to help you:

My self-confidence is affected when . . .
I am encouraged by . . .
When I am criticized by others, I . . .
Sometimes, I am discouraged from . . .
I am motivated to do my best when . . .
My grades are improved when . . .

B **Share** your information with the class.

1 Before you read

Talk with your classmates. Answer the questions.

1. Did you ever feel a lack of self-confidence? What happened?
2. Do your friends or family ever put pressure on you? How?

2 Read

Read the article.

To listen to a recording of the reading, go to www.cambridge.org/transitions

Understanding Self-Confidence

What Is Self-Confidence?

Self-confidence means believing in yourself and your abilities. It means being ready and willing to face new situations and accomplish difficult tasks. Self-confident people are usually eager, assertive, motivated, willing to accept criticism, emotionally mature, optimistic, and productive. People who don't have self-confidence lack the inner belief in their ability to be successful. They tend to be withdrawn, unmotivated, overly sensitive to criticism, distrustful, and pessimistic. They don't feel good about themselves. Often they feel like failures.

What Affects Self-Confidence?

Self-confidence is affected by life experiences. You are influenced by parents, siblings, friends, and teachers. From them, you learn how to think about yourself and the world around you. It is the support and encouragement you receive from the people around you – or the lack of it – that helps shape your inner feelings about yourself.

A nurturing environment that provides positive feedback improves self-confidence. People learn by making mistakes, and they need to feel that missteps along the way are to be expected. However, when friends, family, and others offer unfair criticism, hold unrealistic expectations, or put too much pressure on a person, self-confidence can be affected.

Several different types of behavior show a lack of self-confidence:

1. You judge yourself or your abilities too harshly, or you are overly critical of your performance.

2. You focus too much on your failures and see them as negative events instead of learning experiences.

3. You place too much pressure or stress on yourself to succeed.

4. You set goals that are unrealistic and above your abilities.

5. You are fearful of not succeeding or making mistakes.

A lack of self-confidence can often keep people from achieving their full potential. That's why it's important to get help if you are affected by this problem.

3 After you read

A Check your understanding.

1. People who don't have self-confidence lack some characteristics. What are they?

   _____

2. Name groups of people who influence how you think about yourself.

   _____

3. Name three behaviors that show a lack of self-confidence.

   _____

B Build your vocabulary. Match the words from the reading with their definitions. Use a dictionary to help you.

_c_ 1. motivated (adj.)

____ 2. criticism (n.)

____ 3. influence (v.)

____ 4. stress (n.)

____ 5. succeed (v.)

a. achieve or complete something good that you have been trying to do

b. try to change the way someone thinks or behaves

c. when someone wants to do something

d. a feeling of tension and worry

e. saying that someone or something is bad

Complete the sentences. Use the correct word from the list above.

6. Steve wants to pass the test, but he is tired and needs help to get

   _____ .

7. John's parents had a lot of _____ on how he thinks about

   the world.

8. Ms. Chu wants to _____ and works hard to achieve

   her goals.

9. Lisa puts a lot of pressure on herself and often suffers from

   _____ .

10. Even though Sally is Janet's best friend, Sally often gives her unfair

   _____ .

C Summarize the reading. Work with a partner and take turns restating the main points. Then work together to write a summary. Include the following:

1. definition of self-confidence
2. causes of a lack of self-confidence
3. behavior that shows lack of self-confidence
4. ways to improve self-confidence

Reading

1 Before you read

Talk with your classmates. Answer the questions.

1. The article talks about ways to build self-confidence. What are some things you think it will say?
2. Do you think you are self-confident? Why or why not?

2 Read

Read the article.

To listen to a recording of the reading, go to www.cambridge.org/transitions

Building Self-Confidence

How Do You Build Self-Confidence?

Self-confidence is not built overnight. It is a process that begins by first understanding why you lack confidence, then taking active steps to change your negative thinking and behaviors into positive ones.

First, think about why you lack confidence. Perhaps you are unhappy with your appearance, your social or academic achievements, or the way a relationship ended. Try to identify these feelings and perhaps talk about them with someone you trust. It may surprise you that others share the same kinds of self-doubts or have ones of their own. See your fears as challenges you can overcome – don't let them have power over you!

Steps to Building Self-Confidence

Think of building self-confidence as a process. Aim to make small, positive steps toward success. Practice these strategies until they become your new habits.

1 Think about your good qualities. Are you conscientious, loyal, reliable, and cooperative? Recognize your talents and abilities; these will help you feel better about yourself.

2 Think positively about yourself and what you set out to do. Negative thoughts lead to worry, which can confuse you and keep you from achieving success.

3 Set realistic goals that you can truly reach, both large and small. Praise yourself when you reach even the smallest goals, but keep striving for the bigger ones.

4 Focus on your successes and not on your failures. Realize that everyone makes mistakes, and let yours be tools for learning.

5 Be assertive. It is essential for people to express their thoughts, feelings, and emotions to others. You are entitled to your opinion, and you have important things to say. Don't be afraid to say them.

6 Find a creative outlet for self-expression. Find an activity that lets your abilities shine, such as music, art, cooking, crafts, or sports. You don't have to be the best at what you do, but the risks you take and the things you create provide a fast route to greater self-acceptance.

3 After you read

A Interpret the article. Work with a partner and take turns reading aloud the six strategies for building self-confidence. Then read the descriptions below, and fill in the blank with the number (or numbers) of the strategies that match each example.

_2_ 1. Jessie is applying to be a manager at work. She knows it will be hard at first, but she is focusing on positive things like the opportunity to learn new skills.

_____ 2. Iris was very busy and forgot to register for the class she wanted. She had to sign up for an evening class instead. She knows other students who made the same mistake. Instead of feeling bad about herself, she plans to register early next semester.

_____ 3. Mr. Morales doesn't like his job, but he loves to play guitar. After work every day Mr. Morales spends an hour practicing guitar. This helps him have a positive attitude about himself.

_____ 4. Ali was shy about sharing his ideas in class. Nevertheless, one day he shared his opinion with his classmates. His thoughts helped create an important discussion.

_____ 5. Mrs. Chang feels good about herself even when she has a setback because she knows she is smart and a very hard worker.

B Build your vocabulary.

1. Underline the adjectives from the chart in the reading. Then use a dictionary and write the correct definition to fit the meaning of the word as it's used in the reading.

Vocabulary	Definition
1. conscientious	*showing great care in performing a job or task*
2. reliable	
3. cooperative	
4. assertive	
5. creative	

2. Use the adjectives to write sentences about yourself.

C Summarize the reading. Work with a partner and take turns restating the main points. Then work together to write a summary. Include the following:

1. ways to build self-confidence
2. six steps to building self-confidence

Writing

1 Before you write

A **Talk** with your classmates. Answer the questions.

1. Why do you think employers or schools want to know about your personal strengths?
2. What are your personal strengths?

B **Read** the personal-strength word list. Put a check mark next to the words you know. Put a question mark next to the ones you don't know.

Personal strength words

____ ambitious	____ enthusiastic	____ professional
____ analytical	____ flexible	____ reliable
____ assertive	____ hardworking	____ resourceful
____ attentive	____ knowledgeable	____ responsible
____ cheerful	____ loyal	____ a team player
____ conscientious	____ motivated	____ a troubleshooter
____ dependable	____ organized	____ trustworthy
____ detail-oriented	____ outgoing	
____ diplomatic	____ polite	
____ energetic	____ productive	

C **Talk** with a partner. Write a synonym or definition of the words that are new for you. If necessary, use a dictionary.

2 Write

A **Write.** Look again at the list of personal strength words. Choose two of your best personal strengths from the list and write them down.

Strength #1: _____

Strength #2: _____

B Write. Describe your strengths. Write an example of each strength based on an experience you had.

Example:

Strength: I am enthusiastic. At my last job as a busgirl, even though I didn't earn much money, I was always in a good mood and I did my job well. I was motivated to do a good job. Also, I was friendly to the customers and I made them feel comfortable.

Strength #1: _____

_____

_____

_____

_____

Strength #2: _____

_____

_____

_____

_____

3 After you write

A Check your writing.

	Yes	No
1. I identified two strengths.	☐	☐
2. I gave an example for each strength.	☐	☐
3. I used active and passive verbs correctly.	☐	☐

B Share your writing with a partner.

1. Take turns. Read your writing to a partner.
2. Comment on your partner's writing. Ask your partner questions. Tell your partner one thing you learned.

Get ready

1 Talk about the pictures

A Why do you think many people choose to volunteer?

B Where are the people in the pictures volunteering? Describe each job. If you could choose one of these volunteer jobs, which one would you choose? Why?

Volunteering

2 Listening

A 💿 **Listen** and answer the questions.

1. What was the main idea of the lecture?
2. What are some benefits of volunteering?
3. What are some examples of volunteer opportunities?

B 💿 **Listen again.** Take notes on the key information.

1. Reasons to volunteer
   a.
   b.

2. Examples of volunteer jobs
   a.
   b.
   c.
   d.
   e.

3. Overseas volunteer opportunities
   a.
   b.

Listen again. Check your answers. Did you miss anything important?

C **Exchange** notes with a partner. Do the notes answer the following questions?

1. Why can volunteering be a very beneficial experience?
2. What are some examples of places to volunteer?
3. What are some volunteer jobs that you can do overseas?

D **Discuss.** Talk with your classmates.

1. Are you interested in volunteering? Why or why not?
2. What kind of volunteer work are you good at?
3. How could volunteering help you in the future?

Indirect (reported) speech

1 Grammar focus: Indirect statements

Indirect, or reported, speech is used to report what someone has said. When changing present statements to past, the verbs in both clauses change to past in formal English. Quotation marks are not used.

Direct statements	Indirect statements
"I volunteer at my local school."	She said (that) she volunteered at her local school.
"I'm enjoying my tutoring job."	She said (that) she was enjoying her tutoring job.
"We can't find jobs," they said.	They said (that) they couldn't find jobs.
"I'm not good at carpentry," said Rebecca.	Rebecca said (that) she wasn't good at carpentry.
"I don't like answering phones," Rob said.	Rob said (that) he didn't like answering phones.

2 Practice

A Write. A volunteer coordinator is talking to a person who is interested in volunteering. Change her statements into indirect speech.

1. "Volunteering is a wonderful way to gain experience for a job."

   She said that volunteering was a wonderful way to gain experience for a job.

2. "We have many different types of volunteer jobs."

   _____

3. "Volunteers can work in a school, hospital, nursing home, or library."

   _____

4. "We don't need volunteers at the animal shelter right now."

   _____

5. "It's a good idea to include volunteer experience on a résumé."

   _____

6. "We're looking for several people to help with beach clean-up this weekend."

   _____

B **Talk** with a partner. Discuss what John said about the volunteer positions in the newspaper.

> *A* What did John say about working in an animal shelter?
> *B* He said that he was not really interested in working with animals.

Volunteer positions	What John said
1. Working in an animal shelter	"I'm not really interested in working with animals."
2. Tutoring elementary school students in an after-school reading program	"I prefer to work with adults."
3. Running errands for elderly home-bound (unable to leave home) people	"I like to help elderly people."
4. Building houses for low-income people	"I'm good at building and carpentry."
5. Removing graffiti from public buildings	"I can do this, but I don't want to do it for long periods of time."
6. Preparing food baskets at the local food bank.	"I live too far from the food bank."

Write sentences about John. Use indirect speech.

John said that he was not really interested in working with animals.

3 Communicate

A **Work** with a partner. Role-play conversations between a volunteer coordinator and a university student who is interested in becoming a volunteer.

> *A* What kind of work are you interested in?
> *B* I'm getting my degree in early childhood education, so I want to volunteer with young children.
> *A* We have some volunteer positions working at a day-care center.

B **Perform** your role play for the class.

C **Talk** with your partner. After each role play, report what the counselor and student said. Use indirect speech.

> The student said that she was getting her degree in early childhood education and that she wanted to volunteer with young children. The counselor said that they had some volunteer positions working at a day-care center.

1 Before you read

Talk with your classmates. Answer the questions.

1. Have you and your family ever done any volunteer work together?
2. Does your school have a recycling program? Who runs it?
3. Look at the title. What do you think this article is about?

2 Read

Read the article.

To listen to a recording of the reading,
go to www.cambridge.org/transitions

Community News

Volunteering
the Family Way

For sisters Sarah and Audrey Granger of central Missouri, school and volunteering go hand in hand. Community college sophomore Sarah was recently made Student Coordinator for Recycling at her school – a new, paid position for the college. She immediately started to work by developing a central recycling site, ordering new collection bins for campus buildings, and recruiting her younger sister, Audrey, to be her first volunteer.

Audrey, in her first year at the college, wasn't sure she had time for a volunteer job. With all her classes, she said, she thought it would be too much work. "But after working with Sarah and learning how to collect and organize the material for recycling, I discovered it was easier than I thought," she said.

Because of the instant popularity of the recycling project, Audrey said that she quickly understood the value of her volunteer work. "I started to get the idea that you could make a difference and, after a while, reusing and recycling just became part of my lifestyle."

As coordinator of the campus-wide program, Sarah supervises four volunteers, including her sister. The team has worked hard to introduce recycled paper products in the cafeteria and to use plant waste as compost material in the college's gardens. "It's better to reuse some of the food waste from the cafeteria instead of dumping it in the community landfill," Audrey explained.

For Sarah, who is majoring in environmental studies, the position of Student Coordinator is a perfect way to combine her passion for the environment and her interest in volunteering. She said she became interested in volunteering as a child. "My mother works for Habitat for Humanity," she said, "and I used to spend a lot of time helping her with her projects."

In order to keep the recycling program "going and growing," Sarah said people need to use it and support it as much as possible. With committed volunteers like her sister Audrey, there's no doubt that the program has a bright future.

3 After you read

A Check your understanding.

1. Sarah and Audrey work together at school. How are their duties different?

_____

2. What did Audrey say at first about volunteering?

_____

3. What are two ways recycled products are used at this school?

_____

4. What did Sarah say was necessary for the recycling program to keep "going and growing"?

_____

B Build your vocabulary. Prefixes add meaning to words. Find and underline the words in the reading. Circle the prefixes, then fill in the chart. Use a dictionary if necessary.

Word(s) from reading	Prefix	Meaning of prefix
recycle, reuse	re-	1.
collection	col-	2.
coordinator	co-	3.
supervise	super-	4.
community, combine, committed	com-	5.

Complete the sentences. Write the correct word from the chart.

6. Jorge enjoys working by himself. He does not like to _____ other people.

7. My family likes to _____ Popsicle sticks. We do art projects with them.

8. Mrs. Chavez has a beautiful _____ of glass animals.

9. The students plan to _____ their money and rent a car for a trip to the mountains.

10. James got a new job. He is the new _____ of volunteer projects at the art museum.

C Summarize the reading. Work with a partner and take turns restating the main points. Then work together to write a summary. Include the following:

1. Sarah's job
2. Audrey's job
3. How recycled products are used at the school
4. Sarah's hope for the recycling program

Reading

1 Before you read

Talk with your classmates. Answer the questions.

1. Do you think it is common for college students to volunteer?
2. Should college students volunteer? Why? Why not?

2 Read

Read the article.

To listen to a recording of the reading,
go to www.cambridge.org/transitions

Volunteering
WHILE AT COLLEGE

IT'S NO SECRET that college students have busy lives. Classes, jobs, and studying often leave very little free time for anything else.

Despite their schedules, however, college students are volunteering more than ever, according to a 2006 study by the Corporation for National and Community Services. In fact, the study said college students are more likely to participate in volunteer activities than other people their age not enrolled in college.

There are many benefits to volunteering while in college. First of all, in many states students can get college credit for helping local organizations. In Massachusetts, for example, many students at Holyoke Community College volunteer at community organizations. In return for their good deeds, the students receive credit and are one step closer to graduating.

In order to volunteer for credit, students need to first talk to their advisor. They often need to provide information about the work and the number of hours it will take. The volunteer work is typically related to the student's major.

A second benefit is that volunteering can help satisfy college requirements. At the University of California, Santa Barbara, honor students must volunteer for at least 20 hours during their last two years on campus. This "community-service requirement" is becoming more and more common in schools across the country.

A third benefit to volunteering involves getting a job. Volunteer work looks great on a graduate's résumé. When an employer sees community service on your résumé, it says you want to help others and are curious about the world around you. These characteristics can help get you an interview.

Whether you volunteer for credit, to meet a requirement, or to improve your résumé, keep in mind the most important aspect of community service: making a difference.

3 After you read

A Check your understanding.

1. Who volunteers more, college students or people of the same age not enrolled in college?
2. What are ways that students benefit from volunteering?
3. A college student wants to volunteer for credit. What should he or she do first?
4. What is a community-service requirement?
5. The article suggests putting volunteer work on your résumé. What are two things that volunteering says about you?

B Build your vocabulary. English has many kinds of nouns. For example, verb + -ing forms, called *gerunds*, often have the meaning of actions or processes. Other nouns refer to people. Look at the *gerunds* in the chart. Fill in the related nouns that refer to the person who does the action.

Action	Person
volunteering	1.
studying	2. *student*
helping	3.
graduating	4.
participating	5.

Complete the sentences with a noun from the chart.

6. Joseph got three college credits for ____volunteering____ at the local teen center last semester.

7. My guidance counselor is going to be a _____ in a conference on volunteer opportunities in our community.

8. One day a week Mrs. Flowers is a teacher's _____ in her granddaughter's kindergarten class.

9. My parents came to the United States from Romania. They worked hard and sent me to college. I am the first college _____ in the history of my family.

10. My parents don't want me to work while I am in school. "_____ is your job now, and it's the most important job in the world," they always tell me.

C Summarize the reading. Work with a partner and take turns restating the main points. Then work together to write a summary. Include the following:

1. main idea   2. benefit #1   3. benefit #2   4. benefit #3

1 Before you write

A Talk with a partner. Answer the questions.

1. What are some ways to organize your thoughts before writing?
2. Have you ever used an outline or graphic organizer to plan your writing? How did it help you?

B Look at the graphic organizer. This is an example of *clustering*. It includes the main ideas from the reading in Lesson D, "Volunteering While at College."

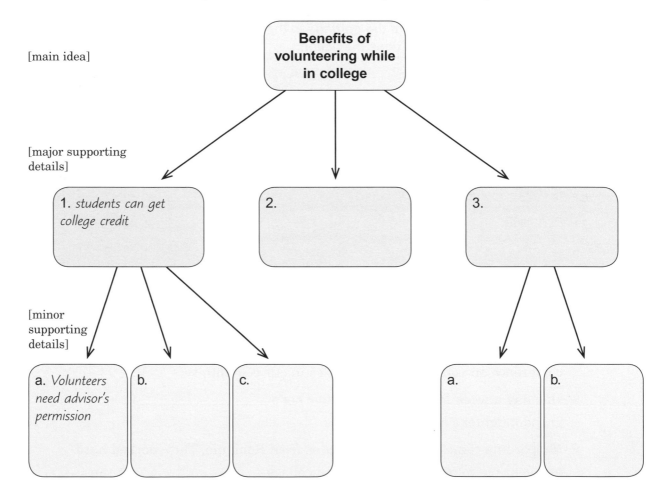

[main idea]

Benefits of volunteering while in college

[major supporting details]

1. students can get college credit

2.

3.

[minor supporting details]

a. Volunteers need advisor's permission

b.

c.

a.

b.

C Work with a partner or partners to complete the chart. Include the key information, but do not write complete sentences. Refer back to the article if you need to.

D **Read** the one-paragraph summary of a two-page government report. Notice these features of the summary:

- The first sentence states the main idea of the article.
- The body sentences summarize the most important supporting details.
- The summary does not include examples.
- Sentences are connected with transitions.
- The summary is paraphrased – written in the writer's words, not the words of the original report.

> A U.S. government report on volunteering in America discussed three major trends in 2009. First, the number of Americans who volunteered through formal organizations increased slightly. In contrast, the number of people who volunteered informally by helping their neighbors or serving their local communities went up dramatically. Finally, there was a significant increase in the number of young adults ages 16–24 who volunteered. The report concluded that today's young people have a strong commitment to serving others.

2 Write

Write a one-paragraph summary of the article "Volunteering While at College." Use Exercises 1B, 1C, and 1D to help you.

3 After you write

A **Check** your writing.

	Yes	No
1. I included the main ideas of the article.	☐	☐
2. I included the reasons people choose to volunteer.	☐	☐
3. I included the ways that volunteering can help you get a job.	☐	☐
4. I did not include unnecessary details in my summary.	☐	☐

B **Share** your writing with a partner.

Effective job applications

1 Talk about the pictures

A What are the people in the pictures doing? What do they need to do next?

B What steps do you need to take when applying for a job?

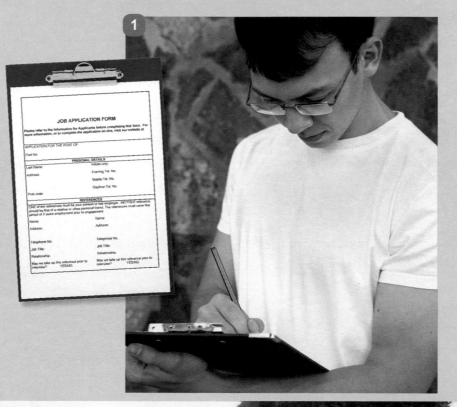

2 Listening

A 🔘 **Listen** and answer the questions.

1. What was the general topic of the lecture?
2. How many steps does the speaker list? Which connecting words told you the order of the steps?

B 🔘 **Listen again.** Take notes on the key information.

> *Steps in finding a job*
> *1.*
>
> *2.*
>
>   *Best way:*
>   *Other ways:*
>
> *3.*
>
>   *Places to find:*
>
> *4.*
>
> *5.*
>
> *6.*
>
> *7. Wait for an invitation for an interview*
>   *While you're waiting:*

Listen again. Check your notes. Did you miss anything important?

C **Discuss.** Talk with your classmates.

1. Have you ever applied for a job? What kind of job was it?
2. Which of the steps in the talk have you tried?
3. Who could you use as a reference for a job you are applying for? Why would this person be a good reference for you?

Lesson A *Get ready*

1 Talk about the pictures

A What are first impressions?

B Why is it important to make a good first impression on the people you meet?

C What are the people in the photographs doing to create a good / bad first impression?

2 Listening

A 🔘 **Listen** and answer the questions.

1. What was the main idea of the talk?
2. What were some interviewing tips that were given in the lecture?

B 🔘 **Listen again.** Take notes on the key information.

Topic: Rules for making a good first impression

Why first impressions are important

 1.

 2.

Rules

 1.

 2.

 3.

 4.

 5.

Listen again. Check your answers. Did you miss anything important?

C **Discuss.** Talk with your classmates.

1. Which of the speaker's five rules have you tried?
2. Which rule is the most important, in your opinion?
3. Are these rules the same or different in your native culture? How?

Reading

1 Before you read

Talk with your classmates. Answer the questions.

1. Have you ever written a thank-you note? In what situation?
2. Why is it important to send a thank-you note after an interview?

2 Read

Read the article.

To listen to a recording of the reading, go to www.cambridge.org/transitions

Make the Most of Your Interview – *Follow Up!*

Let's say you've just had an interview for an on-campus position or with a new company. Now what? Do you just keep checking your e-mail, waiting by the phone, or searching the mail for a letter offering you the position (or not)? Is there anything more you can do to improve the odds of getting the position?

Unfortunately, chances are that there were dozens, if not hundreds, of other applicants for the job or position to which you just applied. And many of the applicants brought the same kinds of skills, experience, and attitude you did to the interview. So the real question is – How do you make yourself stand out from the crowd?

The answer lies in the realization that the interview is not over when you walk out of the interviewer's office. You must follow up.

Sending a thank-you note after your meeting can help you make the most of your interview. A simple note or e-mail thanking the company for considering you for the position or for the chance to meet some of the people involved is a great way to remind the interviewer that you are truly motivated and interested. It also shows that you have good manners.

A thank-you note is appropriate whether or not you felt the interview was successful. If it went well, a thank-you note may persuade the interviewer to select you over other competing candidates. If it did not go well, the note can help the interviewer remember you favorably even if you are not selected.

At the end of your interview, the interviewer should have told you how to follow up and whom to contact. If not, just address the thank-you note to him or her. Write the note soon after the interview to improve the chance that the interviewer will remember you.

It is important to send only *one* follow-up e-mail or note. If you do not get a response, then you can assume you did not get the position. Don't send any more follow-up notes; you will become an annoyance, and that is not your goal.

Instead, be prepared to move on to the next new opportunity. Don't focus on what could have been, but on what may still lie ahead.

3 After you read

A Check your understanding.

1. Why is sending a thank-you note or e-mail important after an interview?
2. Why should you send only one thank-you note as a follow-up?

B Build your vocabulary.

Match the idioms from the reading with their meanings.

Idiom

_____ 1. improve the odds

_____ 2. chances are

_____ 3. stand out from the crowd

_____ 4. make the most of

_____ 5. go well

_____ 6. move on

Meaning

a. change to a new activity

b. succeed

c. it is probably true

d. increase the possibility

e. make it easy for people to remember you

f. take advantage of

Complete the sentences with the best idiom. Change verb forms if necessary.

7. Improving your computer skills will _____ of your getting a good job.

8. My interview with Professor Schmidt _____. I think there is a good chance that he will select me as his research assistant.

9. Teresa _____ of applicants because of her positive attitude.

10. After losing his job, Jorge was depressed for weeks, but eventually he

_____.

11. I don't like my job, but I plan to _____ it.

12. _____ that Gail will move to Washington after she graduates.

C Summarize the reading. Work with a partner and take turns restating the main points. Then work together to write a summary. Try to use the vocabulary from Exercise B. Include the following topics:

1. The importance of an interview follow-up
2. What a thank-you note should say
3. Why, where, and when to send a thank-you note

Writing

1 Before you write

A Talk with a partner. Answer the questions.

1. Are thank-you notes after interviews important in your culture?
2. Have you ever written a thank-you note after an interview? What did it say?

B Read the different ways of expressing gratitude in a thank-you note.

> **Expressing gratitude**
>
> Thank you for . . .
> I'm very grateful for . . .
> I want to express my gratitude/appreciation for . . .
> I appreciate . . .
> I look forward to working with you/talking with you again.

C Read the thank-you e-mail. Underline the expressions of gratitude.

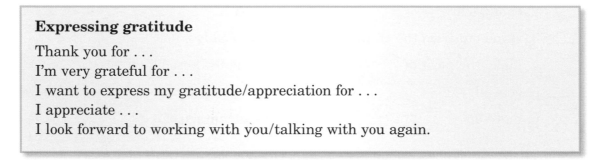

Delete	Junk	Reply	Reply All	Forward	Print	To Do

Subject: Thank you for the interview
From: Ali Bakr
To: Catherine Stevens <c_stevens@cup.org>
Date: February 1, 2012 11:56:23 a.m. PST

Dear Ms. Stevens:

Thank you for inviting me to an interview for the position of afternoon shift manager at La Valle Cafeteria. I enjoyed meeting with you and having the opportunity to tell you about my experience and interest in the position. I also enjoyed the facilities tour and I appreciate the time you spent taking me around. After seeing the kitchen and meeting the student workers, I am excited to think that I might become part of your staff.

Once again, thank you for your help. I look forward to talking with you again soon.

Sincerely,
Ali Bakr

D Plan a thank-you e-mail. Complete the chart below with the information that you will include.

Salutation or greeting	
Statement of thanks (include the position you are applying for)	
Specific details about what you liked about the company, school, or organization	
Repetition of thanks and closing remarks	
Signature	

2 Write

Write a thank-you e-mail. Use the information in Exercises 1B, 1C, and 1D to help you.

3 After you write

A Check your writing.

	Yes	No
1. I included expressions of gratitude.	☐	☐
2. I thanked the interviewer both in the introduction and in the conclusion.	☐	☐
3. I included specific reasons why I liked the interview.	☐	☐

B Share your writing with a partner.

1. Read your partner's note.
2. Who did your partner thank? Why?

Small talk

1 Talk about the pictures

A What is small talk? What are some common small-talk topics in the United States?

B What do you think the people in the photos are talking about?

2 Listening

A **Listen** and answer the questions.

1. What is the purpose of small talk?
2. What are some topics that are appropriate for small talk? What are some topics that are inappropriate?

B **Listen again.** Take notes on the key information.

> Topic:
>
> Definition:
>
>   Examples:
>
> Purposes
>   1.
>
>   2.
>
>
> Appropriate topics:
>
>
> Inappropriate topics:

Listen again. Check your answers. Did you miss anything important?

C **Discuss.** Talk with your classmates.

1. Have you ever listened to Americans making small talk? What did they talk about?
2. In your culture, how do people start a conversation with people they don't know well? Which topics are safe to talk about?

Tag questions

1 Grammar focus: Tag questions

A tag question is a short question that is added to the end of a sentence. Tag questions are used to confirm information or to seek agreement. The tag and the sentence must have the same verb tense. The form is positive sentence + negative tag or negative sentence + positive tag.

Positive sentence + negative tag	Answer	Meaning
It's hot outside, isn't it?	Yes, it is.	You agree that it is hot outside.
You like this class, don't you?	No, I don't.	You disagree. You don't like the class.

Negative sentence + positive tag	Answer	Meaning
Jane hasn't done the homework, has she?	No, she hasn't.	The person who asked the question is correct. Jane has not done the homework.
Lucas didn't get the job, did he?	Yes, he did.	The person who asked the question is mistaken. Lucas got the job.

2 Practice

A Write. Make tag questions and answers using the cues.

1. **A** That was a hard test, _wasn't it_____?

   B _Yes, it was_____. I hope I pass.

2. **A** Meagan works here, _____?

   B _No, she doesn't_____. She works next door.

3. **A** Jim was on Facebook, _____?

   B _____. But he's not anymore.

4. **A** Lida hasn't seen the movie before, _____?

   B _____. She is waiting until she can rent the DVD.

5. **A** You're going to the meeting, _____?

   B _____. But I have to leave early.

6. **A** This wasn't written by you, _____?

   B _____. Cindy wrote it.

7. **A** You're not from Argentina, _____?

   B _____, actually. I'm from Buenos Aires.

B Talk with a partner. Make small talk by asking and answering tag questions.

> A You're from Korea, aren't you?
> B No, I'm not. I'm from Thailand.

Student A

You think that your partner . . .

1. is from _____ (country)
2. came to the United States last year
3. is married
4. has two children
5. didn't come to class yesterday
6. is going to work right after class
7. can't speak Spanish
8. will be in class tomorrow

Student B

You think that your partner . . .

1. is from _____ (country)
2. just bought a car
3. isn't married
4. has a dog
5. didn't go to work yesterday
6. is going to move to _____ (state)
7. can't sing
8. is leaving early today

3 Communicate

A Write six sentences about yourself – three that are true and three that are not true. Exchange papers with a partner. Use your partner's sentences to ask tag questions. Answer your partner's questions.

B Work with a partner. Role-play a conversation between two people who are making small talk at a party. Begin with a tag question. End the conversation politely. Begin your conversation with a comment about one of these topics:

- the weather or room temperature
- the party, the room, the food, the host, or the music
- where you've seen the other person before

> A It's hot in here, isn't it?
> B Yes, it sure is.
> A Are you from around here?
> B No, I'm actually from _____.
> A Me, too. We have a lot to talk about!
> B Oh, I'd love to continue this conversation, but I've got to go now.
> A Oh, sorry to hear that. Take care.
> B Bye!

C Perform your role play for the class.

1 Before you read

Talk with your classmates. Answer the questions.

1. The article below is called "Small Talk, Big Problems." What do you think it's about?
2. Have you ever had problems with understanding small talk?

2 Read

Read the article.

To listen to a recording of the reading, go to www.cambridge.org/transitions

Small Talk, Big Problems

MARCO, A NEW IMMIGRANT FROM CHILE, works in a factory during the day and takes college classes at night. Shortly after starting at work and at school, he has two confusing experiences:

- One evening, he sees an American student from one of his classes walking toward him. As the student comes closer, Marco says, "Hi." The student responds with "Hi, how are you?" But instead of waiting for Marco's answer, the student keeps on walking. Marco is confused and wonders, "Why does my classmate dislike me?"
- At the factory, Marco sits down to have lunch with a group of co-workers. He introduces himself and talks a bit about his family, and his co-workers do the same. At the end of lunch, an American co-worker says, "It was nice to meet you, Marco. Let's get together sometime." A week goes by. Marco sees the woman every day, but she never talks about seeing him or getting together with him outside of work. Marco wonders, "Why did she lie to me?"

Are Marco's conclusions correct? Does his classmate dislike him? Is his co-worker a liar? In both cases, no. Neither the classmate nor the colleague was trying to be rude.

The problem in these scenarios was that Marco was unaware of the difference between the speakers' *words* and their *intentions*. Marco did not know that "How are you?" "Let's get together," and similar expressions are actually a form of small talk. "How are you?" and "How are you doing?" are not real questions. They are greetings, similar to "Hello." A speaker who uses these expressions does not expect an answer beyond "Fine, thanks."

Likewise, "Let's keep in touch," "I'll call you," or "Let's talk soon" are not invitations or promises to get in touch. They are simply polite ways of closing a conversation.

But if Americans don't mean what they say, how can you know when they are truly interested in knowing about your health or when they're sincerely looking forward to meeting you again? Watch their behavior. If the speaker makes eye contact and waits to hear your answer, chances are they are asking a real question. In the second case, you can recognize a real invitation if the speaker makes an appointment with you for a specific day and time.

The lesson to learn from Marco's experiences is that it isn't always enough to understand the words that people use. You have to know the intention, or purpose, behind them as well.

3 After you read

A Check your understanding.

1. What was the cause of Marco's misunderstandings?
2. What are some examples of small talk phrases that are often misunderstood?
3. How should you respond if an American says "How are you?" or "Let's keep in touch."

B Build your vocabulary.

1. English has many verb + preposition + -ing combinations. It can be difficult to remember which prepositions to use. Fill in the missing prepositions in the combinations below. Then write an explanation or synonym for each combination. Use a dictionary if necessary.

Preposition Combination	Definition
1. keep _____ (walking)	*continue*
2. talk _____ (seeing)	
3. be guilty _____ (lying)	
4. be interested _____ (knowing)	
5. look forward _____ (meeting)	

2. Write your own sentences with the verb + preposition + -ing combinations.

C Summarize the reading. Work with a partner and take turns restating the main points. Then work together to write a summary. Try to use the vocabulary from Exercise B. Include the following topics:

1. the cause of Marco's misunderstandings
2. examples of expressions that don't mean what they sound like
3. how to know when Americans mean what they say
4. the lesson to learn from Marco's experiences

Lesson E *Writing*

1 Before you write

A Talk with your classmates. Answer the questions.

1. Review what you learned in Lesson A (page 53) about appropriate and inappropriate topics for small talk in the United States. Give examples of questions you should and shouldn't ask.

2. How is small talk in your country the same as in the United States? How is it different?

B Make a list in your notebook of appropriate and inappropriate small-talk topics in your culture.

C Complete the diagrams.

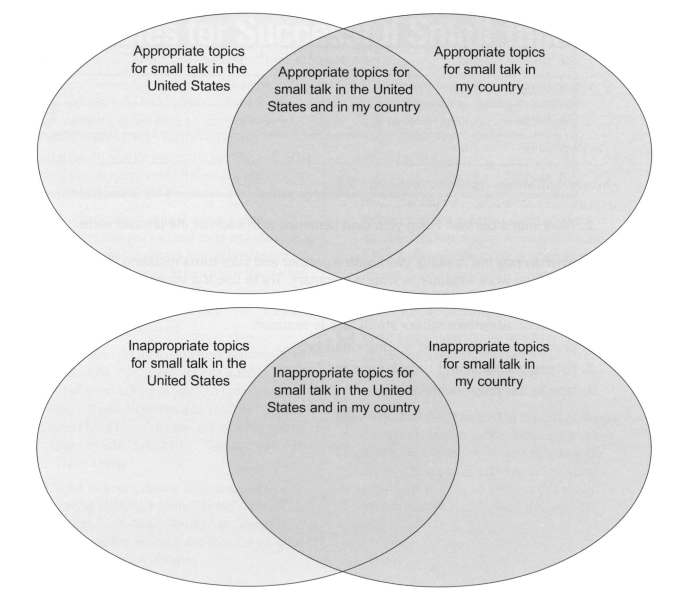

Appropriate topics for small talk in the United States

Appropriate topics for small talk in the United States and in my country

Appropriate topics for small talk in my country

Inappropriate topics for small talk in the United States

Inappropriate topics for small talk in the United States and in my country

Inappropriate topics for small talk in my country

D Plan a paragraph comparing appropriate and inappropriate topics for small talk in the United States and in your country. Use the outline in the chart as a guide; you may change words and add or delete topics or examples according to the information you want to include.

Topic sentence	*Appropriate and inappropriate small talk topics in the United States and _____ (your country) are mostly (similar / different).*
Similarities	• topics that are appropriate in both cultures • examples of common questions
Differences	• topics that are inappropriate in the United States, but acceptable in my culture • examples
	• topics that are appropriate in the United States, but unacceptable in my culture • examples
Conclusion	*These are just a few examples of how small talk topics are similar and different in the United States and in my country.*

2 Write

Write a paragraph comparing appropriate and inappropriate topics for small talk in the United States and in your country. Use Exercises 1A, 1B, 1C, and 1D to help you.

3 After you write

A Check your writing

	Yes	No
1. I wrote a topic sentence expressing my main idea.	☐	☐
2. I wrote about similarities between the United States and my country.	☐	☐
3. I wrote about differences between the United States and my country.	☐	☐
4. I wrote a conclusion for my paragraph.	☐	☐

B Share your writing with a partner.

1. Take turns. Read your writing to your partner.
2. Comment on your partner's writing. Ask your partner questions. Tell your partner one thing you learned.

Get ready

Improving relationships

1 Talk about the pictures

A Are the people in the pictures working alone or in groups? Is this the best way for them to work, in your opinion?

B What is teamwork? Why is it important at work and school?

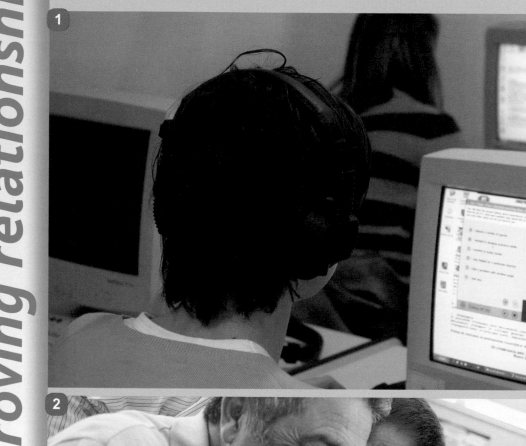

2 Listening

A 💿 **Listen** and answer the questions.

1. What is the definition of teamwork?
2. Why is teamwork important?
3. According to the speaker, what is one benefit of teamwork?

B 💿 **Listen again.** Take notes on the key information.

Topic:

Definition:

Importance

    For organizations:

    For individuals:

Benefits

    1. Increased employee/student involvement

    2.

    3.

    4.

Conclusion

    In the past:

    Today:

Listen again. Check your notes. Did you miss anything important?

C Discuss. Talk with your classmates.

1. Why do you think teamwork reduces absenteeism?
2. How do you think teamwork reduces costs in an organization?
3. In your country, is it common for students and workers to work in teams?
4. Do you enjoy working on teams at school or work? Why or why not?

Unreal conditionals

1 Grammar focus: The present unreal conditional

Conditional sentences consist of a dependent clause and a main clause. The dependent clause begins with *if*. The main clause uses *would*, *could*, or *might* + verb. Use the present unreal conditional to talk about imaginary situations in the present or to give advice. Use a comma after an *if*-clause at the beginning of a sentence.

Example	Explanation
If we had more time, we could do a better job.	We don't have enough time, so we can't do a good job.
We could finish this project faster if we had more people on our team.	We don't have enough people on our team, so we can't work quickly.
If I were you, I would talk to the boss about the problem.	You should talk to the boss about the problem.
	In formal English, the form of the *be*-verb in the dependent clause is *were* for all subjects. In conversation it is acceptable to say *If I was* or *If he/she was*.

2 Practice

A **Write.** Complete the sentences. Use the present unreal conditional. Use *would*, *could*, or *might* in the main clause.

1. At the ZZ Mattress Company, we don't work in teams. If we (work) _____worked_____ in teams, we (save) _____might save_____ time.

2. We don't have enough space in our office. Maybe the workers (be) _____ more patient with each other if we (have) _____ more space.

3. My office mate talks on his cell phone all the time. I (concentrate) _____ better if he (talk) _____ outside.

4. Our manager is not a good communicator. If our manager (be) _____ a better communicator, we (not have) _____ trouble following directions.

5. Jim's manager does not trust him. Jim (be) _____ more motivated to work hard if his manager (trust) _____ him.

6. I'm sorry you're having problems with your team leader. If I (be) _____ you, I (join) _____ a different team.

7. Carmen does not work well in teams. If I (be) _____ her manager, I (not force) _____ her to work with other people.

B Talk with a partner. Read the paragraph and the sentences about Peter. Make sentences about the imaginary situations. Use the present unreal conditional.

Peter is a teaching assistant in a large class. He got the job because he is smart and he knows the material well. But there are several problems in his class.

Peter is shy, so he doesn't relate well to the students.

> But if he weren't shy, he could relate well to the students.

1. He speaks softly, so the students can't hear him.
2. He never asks any questions, so the students don't need to pay attention.
3. He does not use interesting examples, so his lectures are boring.
4. The students don't respect him, so they come to class late.
5. There are no rules for behavior, so the students use their cell phones and text during class.
6. His tests are easy, so the students are not challenged.
7. His department chair never observes his class, so she doesn't know about the problems.

Write sentences about Peter. Use the present unreal conditional.

If Peter spoke more loudly, the students could hear him.

3 Communicate

Work in small groups. Take turns reading the situations and giving advice. Use *If I were you . . .* for advice.

1. You and three other students are assigned to do a research project for your business class. One student in the group is not doing his share of the work. You're worried that your project will be late because of him, and you will get a lower grade.

> If I were you, I would speak to the professor about the problem.

2. You're working with a committee to plan a dinner honoring your children's teacher, who is retiring. One person on the committee is very bossy. She is always telling everyone else what to do. You like this woman, but it's hard for you to work with her.

3. Your boss assigned a project to you and three other workers. He gave you a deadline, but no directions about how to divide up the work. You've never worked on a team before, and you don't know how to begin.

1 Before you read

Talk with your classmates. Answer the questions.

1. What are some annoying or disruptive behaviors at work or in school?
2. Who is responsible for protecting students or workers from disruptive or abusive behavior?

2 Read

Read the article.

To listen to a recording of the reading, go to www.cambridge.org/transitions

Bad Behavior in the Workplace

A recent survey by Randstad USA, an employer staffing firm, asked over 1,500 U.S. employees to identify the things co-workers do that they find most annoying. Number one on the list of the seven worst behaviors was gossiping, the passing around of rumors and intimate information.

Other employee pet peeves included wasting company time with poor time-management skills, colleagues who leave messes in common areas such as the lunch or meeting rooms, unpleasant scents and loud noises in the office, overuse of phones and laptops in meetings, and misuse of company e-mail (for example, e-mailing too often or copying too many people on messages).

But the list of bothersome behaviors in the workplace did not end there. It included abusive behaviors like bullying and sexual harassment. An earlier survey done by the online learning provider SkillSoft found bullying by co-workers and management to be a top employee concern.

"Bullying" is defined as behavior done by a person with greater power for the purpose of intimidating, or frightening, a weaker or less powerful person. The term "bully" is usually associated with a child who behaves badly, but a manager who repeatedly criticizes a worker in front of co-workers, or a professor who ridicules a student's religious beliefs or appearance, may also be guilty of bullying.

Sexual harassment – which includes inappropriate touching or sexual remarks and using threats to force unwanted sexual activity on an employee or fellow student – is a serious workplace abuse. Both males and females can be targets of sexual harassment.

Both bullying and sexual harassment are against the law. All government and state offices, as well as colleges, have written policies that define and prohibit these behaviors. So do most large companies. The U.S. Equal Employment Opportunity Commission, or EEOC, is the government agency in charge of enforcing laws against discrimination, which includes sexual harassment.

Annoying colleagues, bad work etiquette, and abusive behavior can all lead to unhappy working conditions that affect worker productivity and satisfaction. Well-managed organizations have rules and procedures in place to define improper behavior and prevent these abuses.

3 After you read

A Check your understanding.

1. What are some examples of employee pet peeves? Do these things annoy you, too?
2. What is an example of bullying at work? Can you think of any others?
3. What advice would you give a classmate who was being bullied? Start with "If I were you . . ."
4. What is sexual harassment?

B Build your vocabulary.

1. English uses punctuation, phrases, and clauses to signal definitions in a text. Look for the following expressions in the reading and complete the chart.

Expression	Definition signal	Definition
1. gossiping	*a comma between two nouns ("gossiping" and "passing")*	*the passing around of rumors and intimate information*
2. pet peeves		
3. common areas		
4. misuse of company e-mail		
5. abusive behaviors		
6. bullying		
7. intimidating		
8. sexual harassment		

2. Use each expression from the chart in an original sentence about your workplace, school, or volunteer organization.

C Summarize the reading. Work with a partner and take turns restating the main points. Then work together to write a summary. Try to use the vocabulary from Exercise B. Include the following topics:

1. findings of the Randstad USA survey
2. finding of the SkillSoft study
3. examples of bullying and sexual harassment
4. the EEOC

1 Before you read

Talk with your classmates. Answer the questions.

1. Has anyone ever annoyed you at work or school? How did you deal with it?
2. What do you think is the best way to deal with annoying people?

2 Read

Read the article.

To listen to a recording of the reading, go to www.cambridge.org/transitions

Don't Let Annoying People Drive You Nuts

How many times have you had to put up with a phone ringing in someone's pocket in class, the loud talker in the seat behind you on a plane, or the choking smell of perfume in the office meeting room? When someone's behavior annoys you, what do you do? Well, if you don't know the offending person or aren't tied to the situation, you can get up and leave. But what if you can't leave, or if you're forced to share space with a person who regularly drives you up a wall – what then?

Getting Angry Isn't the Answer

Experts in group relations say that getting angry with an annoying person only makes a bad situation worse. A confrontation can put you in a bad mood, increase your stress level, and make you say things that you might regret later. However, turning a blind eye to the problem and doing nothing will only make you more resentful, and it won't make things better.

The Direct Approach Is Often the Best

If you decide the problem is bad enough, and if you can't avoid it by changing office desks or moving to a different part of the classroom, many experts agree that addressing the problem head-on is your best approach. But be careful.

If you sound overly critical or accusatory, your attempt to clear the air might backfire and make matters worse.

Instead of criticizing, experts suggest a more constructive approach. First, try to take into account the other person's feelings. He or she may not be aware of their annoying behavior. Just letting the person know your point of view – without criticizing or putting blame on them – is a healthy approach. Use "I" language instead of "you" language. For example, saying "I would appreciate you keeping your voice down a little" sounds much less accusatory and mean-spirited than "You talk so loud, I can't hear myself think."

If the annoyance is minor, like a colleague whose gum chewing grates on your nerves, don't make a big deal out of it. An indirect or joking comment may be sufficient: "Hey, I guess that gum tastes really good! But I'm having trouble concentrating – could you please chew more quietly?"

In short, when it comes to dealing with annoying classmates or co-workers, a little diplomacy goes a long way.

3 After you read

A Check your understanding.

1. Why is it not helpful to get angry with annoying people?
2. What does the writer mean by a "direct" approach?
3. What is "I" language? Give an example.
4. A friend is annoyed with a colleague who often uses office e-mail to send around photos of her family. What advice would you give your friend? Start with "If I were you . . ."

B Build your vocabulary.

1. Complete the idioms in the chart using words from the reading.

2. Work with a partner. Write a synonym or explanation for each idiom.

Idiom	Explanation
1. _____drive_____ you nuts	To irritate or annoy very much
2. drive you up a _____	
3. in a bad _____	
4. turning a _____ eye	
5. address a problem _____ on	
6. clear the _____	
7. take into _____	
8. grate on your _____	
9. make a big _____ out of something	

3. Work with your partner to write a short conversation. Use two idioms from the chart. Role-play your conversation with the class.

C Summarize the reading. Work with a partner and take turns restating the main points. Then work together to write a summary. Try to use the vocabulary from Exercise B. Include the following topics:

1. examples of annoying behaviors
2. why you shouldn't get angry
3. ways of approaching annoying people in a positive way

1 Before you write

A **Talk** with your classmates. Answer the questions.

1. Do you ever read advice columns in newspapers, magazines, or online?

2. Have you ever written a letter asking for advice? Did you get a response? Did you follow the advice you received?

B **Read** the letter and response in a workplace advice column.

WORKPLACE ADVICE

Dear Brenda,

I have an embarrassing problem. I really don't know how to deal with it. My office mate has very strong body odor. It has gotten to the point where I cannot stand to be in my office anymore. I have tried leaving the door open, but it doesn't work. I've been spending most of my day in the next office, but this is not ideal because I feel like I am crowding out the people who work there. My co-worker is a very nice person. What would you do if you were me?

— Desperate for Air, New York, NY

Dear Desperate,

That situation sounds very awkward. No one likes to hear that they smell bad. If I were you, I would put together a nice package of personal cleansing items like soap, deodorant, and a washcloth. I would wrap the package and give it to my office mate as a gift. I would explain that I am very sensitive to strong smells, and that I would appreciate it if she used these items. Try to speak gently and calmly. Explain that you enjoy sharing an office with her, and that this will help you work together better. If this solution does not work, ask your supervisor to move you to a different office. Explain that your current office environment is interfering with your ability to concentrate on your work. I respect your effort to take your office mate's feelings into account, but your first responsibility is to perform your job duties as effectively as possible.

— Brenda

C **Work** with a partner. Answer the questions about Brenda's response.

1. What information does the advice columnist write at the beginning of her response?

2. How many solutions does the advice columnist suggest?

3. What grammar and expressions does the columnist use to give advice?

D Plan a response to a letter asking for advice about an annoying problem at work or school.

1. Choose a problem to respond to. It can be a real problem you've had at work or school, or it can be one of the problems in the readings on pages 66 and 68. Summarize the problem here:

_____

_____

_____

_____

_____

2. Imagine you are an advice columnist. Brainstorm solutions to the problem.

Solution 1: _____

_____

Solution 2: _____

_____

Solution 3: _____

_____

2 Write

Write a paragraph in which you respond to a letter asking for advice about an annoying problem at school or work. Include at least two solutions. Use Exercises 1B, 1C, and 1D to help you.

3 After you write

A Check your writing.

	Yes	No
1. I referred to the problem in the first one or two sentences of my response.	☐	☐
2. I suggested at least two solutions.	☐	☐
3. I used *If I were you* and imperative verbs to give advice.	☐	☐

B Share your writing with a partner.

1. Take turns. Explain the problem to your partner. Then read your response.
2. Respond to your partner's writing. Do you agree with the advice your partner gave?

Giving and receiving criticism

1 Talk about the pictures

A What is criticism? Is criticism always negative?

B What kind of criticism do you think the people in the photos received?

2 Listening

A 💿 **Listen** and answer the questions.

1. Who criticized Ray? Why? How?
2. What was Ray's response?
3. What is the difference between negative criticism and constructive criticism?

B 💿 **Listen again.** Take notes on the key information.

Topic:

Ray's story

    Test grade:

    Professor's written comment:

    Comments to Ray in office:

    Ray's reaction:

Consequences of negative criticism:

How to give constructive criticism:

Listen again. Check your answers. Did you miss anything important?

C **Discuss.** Talk with your classmates.

1. According to the three steps of giving constructive criticism, what should Ray's professor have done differently?
2. Have you ever been in a situation where you felt you were criticized unfairly? What did you do to resolve the situation?

Lesson B *Conditional clauses*

1 Grammar focus: Past unreal conditional

The past unreal conditional expresses opinions or wishes about situations that were unreal (not true) in the past. The verb forms are *had* + past participle in the dependent clause and *would / could / might (not)* + *have* + past participle in the main clause. Use a comma after an *if*-clause at the beginning of a sentence.

Example	Explanation
If Ray had studied more for the test, he would have gotten a higher score.	Ray got a low score on the test because he didn't study enough.
Ray wouldn't have done so badly on the test if he had gone to a study session.	Ray didn't go to a study session. He did badly on the test.

2 Practice

A Write. Complete the sentences. Use the past unreal conditional.

1. Tom didn't receive the e-mail about the staff meeting, so he didn't go. If Tom (receive) ____*had received*____ the e-mail, he (go) __*would have gone*__ to the meeting.

2. Donna forgot to put gas in her car. She ran out of gas and was late to class. She (not be) _____ late if she (remember) _____ to put gas in her car.

3. Steve turned in his paper late. He got a bad grade. Steve (get) _____ a better grade if he (turn in) _____ his paper on time.

4. Tina wrote her report too quickly. Her boss made her rewrite it. If Tina (write) _____ her report more carefully, her boss (not make) _____ her do it again.

5. Jim yelled at his boss. His boss got upset. If Jim (not yell) _____ at his boss, his boss (not get) _____ upset.

6. Jack needed more time to finish his project. He asked Boutros to help him. He (not finish) _____ the project on time if Boutros (not help) _____ him.

7. George's English class didn't have a year-end party. The students didn't get a chance to say good-bye to each other. If the class (have) _____ a year-end party, the students (have) _____ a chance to say good-bye.

B **Talk** with a partner. Read about Mario. Use the cues to make sentences about what would or could have happened if the situation had been different.

Mario recently got a job in a busy office. The work is challenging, but Mario is satisfied because he's learning new skills. His boss is demanding but fair.

Yesterday Mario had a hard day. His boss assigned him an important project to do by himself.

> If the boss hadn't trusted Mario, he wouldn't have assigned him an important project.

1. The boss trusted Mario, so he assigned him an important project.
2. The project had a tight deadline. Mario worried about finishing on time.
3. Mario didn't feel confident because he didn't have a colleague to consult.
4. Mario needed to work overtime because there were problems.
5. Mario's desk was full of papers, so he lost an important document.
6. Mario's computer crashed, so he lost some data.
7. Mario finished the project on time because he stayed up all night.
8. The boss was pleased because Mario finished the project on time.

Write sentences about Mario. Use the past unreal conditional.

If the boss hadn't trusted Mario, he wouldn't have assigned him an important project.

3 Communicate

A **Write** a list of five things you are sorry that you did or did not do at work or school. Say what happened as a result.

I lent my lecture notes to Linda and she lost them.

B **Work** with a partner. Take turns reading and responding to your sentences from A. Use the past unreal conditional in your responses.

> *A* I lent my lecture notes to Linda and she lost them.
> *B* That's too bad. If you hadn't lent your notes to Linda, she wouldn't have lost them.
> *A* You're right. In the future I won't lend my notes to anyone.

C **Share** information about your partner with the class.

1 Before you read

Talk with your classmates. Answer the questions.

1. What do you think "accepting criticism gracefully" means?
2. Why is it important to accept criticism this way?

2 Read

Read the article.

To listen to a recording of the reading, go to www.cambridge.org/transitions

Accepting Criticism Gracefully

Accepting criticism gracefully is not an easy thing to do. Criticism can be extremely hurtful and can make us feel exposed and vulnerable. In her article "Handling Criticism with Honesty and Grace," communications expert Kare Anderson offers some insights into why criticism makes us feel so bad and how to lessen the pain.

Anderson states that criticism is so powerful because when we receive it, we are like animals under attack. "Your heart beats faster [and] your skin temperature goes down . . . your instincts are to focus on that feeling," which makes it stronger. Criticism, she adds, makes people want to either run away or fight back.

Anderson says it is important to focus on the content of the critical comments and not to let defensive emotions build up inside us. Putting up defenses may lead us to take "a superior or righteous position, get more rigid, and listen less as the criticism continues."

Anderson encourages people to follow a four-step process when responding to criticism.

1 Step one is to show, either verbally or with a simple nod, that you heard the criticism. Staying calm and saying something like "I understand how concerned you are about this" is much better than saying "You are totally wrong" or "You don't know what you are talking about."

2 Step two is to ask for more information, even if you disagree with the criticism. This will help both parties understand the message. Anderson says, "The more fully the [critical] person feels heard, the more likely he or she will be receptive to your response."

3 In step three, both parties should seek to find something they can agree on in the message. Usually there is some kernel of truth in criticism. Take responsibility for at least that much. If there is nothing at all to agree upon, however, look at the positive intentions of the critical party, saying something like "I understand your need to be very thorough." or "If I had known how much you cared about the project, . . ."

4 Step four is responding to the criticism, but always after asking permission first. If you disagree with the criticism, you can say, "May I give you my opinion?" or "What can we do to make things better?" However, Anderson says, "if [on the other hand] you believe the [critical] comments are accurate, say so. If an apology is in order, give it sooner rather than later."

3 After you read

A Check your understanding.

1. How do most people typically feel when someone criticizes them?
2. When someone criticizes you, why is it important to focus on the content of the criticism?
3. What steps should people follow when responding to criticism, according to Anderson?
4. Imagine your teacher criticized your essay because it is too long. You disagree. What could you say to your teacher according to each of Anderson's four steps?

B Build your vocabulary.

1. Read the words in the chart that end in *-ly*. These words are *adverbs*. They modify verbs, adjectives, other adverbs, and whole sentences.

2. Find and underline the expressions with adverbs in the reading. In the chart, check the form that the adverbs modify.

	Verb	Adjective	Adverb	Whole sentence
1. accepting criticism *gracefully*	✓			
2. *extremely* hurtful				
3. show *verbally*				
4. you are *totally* wrong				
5. the more *fully* the person feels heard				
6. *Usually* there is some kernel				

3. Work with a partner. Choose one adverb from the chart and form your own sentence in which the adverb modifies a verb, an adjective, another adverb, or a whole sentence.

C Summarize the reading. Work with a partner and take turns restating the main points. Then work together to write a summary. Try to use the vocabulary from Exercise B. Include the following topics:

1. why criticism affects people strongly
2. the four steps of receiving and responding to criticism
3. the importance of focusing on the message – not your feelings

1 Before you read

Talk with your classmates. Answer the questions.

1. In which situations do people normally receive evaluations (written or spoken) of their performance?
2. Have you ever had a performance evaluation? In which situation? How did you deal with criticism, if any?

2 Read

Read the article.

To listen to a recording of the reading, go to www.cambridge.org/transitions

The Performance Evaluation

Serena was sitting in the office cafeteria reading the newspaper when her friend John walked in. He looked rather sad. John poured himself a cup of coffee and walked over to her. "Hi," he said, slumping down into a chair.

Serena looked up from her paper. "Looks like things didn't go well with your evaluation," she said.

"Nope, it was awful."

"What happened?" she asked.

"I messed up," said John. "I lost my cool when Bill said some things about my performance I didn't agree with."

"Why did you do that?" asked Serena.

"I don't know really. I felt hurt, I guess, and embarrassed."

Serena put down her paper. "What exactly did he say?"

"Well, first," said John, "he said I need to use my time better, you know, stop chitchatting so much with co-workers because I wasn't working fast enough." John looked up at her. "Just hearing it started my heart racing and all I could think about was how bad it made me feel. Then he said a few more negative things."

"What more did he say?"

"You know," answered John, "I'm not really sure. I can't remember now."

"You can't remember . . . weren't you listening?" asked Serena.

"Well, yes and no . . . you see, I started to get all defensive and started talking about what a good job I do and how much I disagreed with him." John shook his head. "Then I started blabbing about my workload and how the other folks in my department aren't pulling their weight."

"You started blaming others?" said Serena.

"Yeah, I know," John said, looking over at her. "Bad, huh?" He drank his coffee and stared into his cup. "I was so surprised and embarrassed, I just blew up."

John thought for a moment, then said, "I wish I could do it over again. If I had known he was so displeased with my work, I would have been more prepared for the criticism. Maybe I would have been more calm."

John suddenly stood up.

"Where are you going?" asked Serena.

"First I'm going to e-mail Bill an apology and ask for another meeting," he said, sliding his chair beneath the table, "and then I'm getting back to work."

3 After you read

A Check your understanding.

1. What did Bill say about John's performance?
2. How did John react to his boss's criticism?
3. If John had known that his boss was displeased, how would he have behaved differently?
4. What is John going to do next?

B Build your vocabulary.

1. The expressions in the chart are examples of *slang*, or informal language. Slang is common in casual conversation; you should not use it in formal speaking situations or when you write. Look for the expressions in the reading and underline them.

2. Look up the expressions in a dictionary. Write formal synonyms or definitions in the chart.

Slang expression	Formal synonym/definition
1. nope	*no*
2. mess up	
3. lose one's cool	
4. chitchat	
5. blab	
6. pull one's weight	
7. blow up	

3. Work with a partner. Role-play short conversations (two or three lines) using the slang expressions. Then write sentences using the formal synonyms.

C Summarize the reading. Work with a partner and take turns restating the main points. Then work together to write a summary. Try to use the vocabulary from Exercise B. Include the following topics:

1. Bill's criticism of John's performance
2. how John felt
3. what John said
4. John's feelings now
5. what John plans to do next

Writing

1 Before you write

A Talk with your classmates. Answer the questions.

1. Think of a time when you received criticism. Who criticized you – a teacher, a supervisor, a family member, an acquaintance, or a stranger?
2. Was the criticism negative or constructive?
3. How did you react to the criticism?
4. Did you change as a result of the criticism? How?

B Read the story.

An Educational Experience

The summer after I graduated from high school I traveled to Paris, France.

I had studied French for three years in high school and I had always gotten good grades. I thought my French was pretty good, and I was very excited about going to France and trying out the language there. On my first day, I went to a café and ordered a café au lait. As soon as the waiter heard my French, he started to laugh and make jokes about Americans and their funny accents. I was devastated. I got so flustered that I couldn't remember another word in French. I had to hold back my tears.

For several days after that I refused to speak French. But gradually, I realized that I could have handled the situation differently. I could have laughed at myself along with the waiter. I made up my mind to listen carefully to the way French people speak and to try to imitate their accent. I began to speak French again, and I didn't let people's comments about my accent bother me.

I realize now that the waiter was very rude to laugh at me, but I also realize that he did me a favor. Today I speak fluent French with a very good accent. If that waiter hadn't criticized me, I probably wouldn't have improved as much as I did.

C Work with a partner. Answer the questions.

1. Where and when did the story take place?
2. Who criticized the writer? What did she do or say? Was the criticism constructive or negative?
3. How did the writer feel?
4. How did the writer respond?
5. What could the writer have done differently?
6. How did the writer change, or what did she learn, as a result of the criticism?

D Plan a story about a time when someone criticized you, either constructively or negatively. Outline the story on your own paper. Include answers to questions similar to those in Exercise 1C in your outline.

2 Write

Write the story about the time when someone criticized you, how you responded, and what you learned from the experience. Use Exercises 1A, 1B, and 1C to help you.

3 After you write

A Check your writing.

	Yes	No
1. I wrote about who criticized me, where it happened, when it happened, and what the person said.	☐	☐
2. I described how I felt and how I responded.	☐	☐
3. I used past modals or the past unreal conditional to talk about what I should have done differently.	☐	☐
4. I wrote about what I learned or how I changed as a result of the criticism.	☐	☐

B Share your writing with a partner.

1. Take turns. Read your partner's story.
2. Comment on your partner's writing. Ask your partner a question. Tell your partner one thing you learned.

The right attitude

1 Talk about the pictures

A What does it mean to have a positive or a negative attitude? Give examples.

B Do you think the people in the photos have a positive or a negative attitude? Why do you think so?

2 Listening

A 🔘 **Listen** and answer the questions.

1. Who is the speaker in this talk? Who are the listeners? Why are they there?

2. Which behaviors can show whether a person has a positive or a negative attitude?

B 🔘 **Listen again.** Take notes on the key information.

Topic:

Behaviors of positive people:

Behaviors of negative people:

Listen again. Check your notes. Did you miss anything important?

C **Discuss.** Talk with your classmates.

1. Describe some positive and negative people you know. How do they behave?

2. What causes some people to have a negative attitude?

3. What can a person do to change a negative attitude?

Adverb clauses of concession

1 Grammar focus: *Although* and *Even though*

Adverb clauses with *although* and *even though* are called concession clauses. These words signal that the information in the main clause is surprising or unexpected. The dependent clause can go at the beginning or at the end of the sentence. A comma is used if it is at the beginning.

Although Beth is usually a positive person, she sometimes complains about her job.

Beth sometimes complains about her job although she is a positive person.

Even though your courses are stressful sometimes, try to have a positive attitude.

Try to have a positive attitude even though your courses are stressful sometimes.

2 Practice

A **Write.** Choose the best clause to complete each sentence. Then write the sentence. Insert a comma if necessary.

1. Mike has a great job.
   a. he complains about his work all the time   b. he really likes his boss

   Although *Mike has a great job, he complains about his work all the time.*

2. Susan still feels stressed out.
   a. she goes to stress reduction classes   b. she is starting to feel better

   _____ even though _____

3. John is a positive example for his staff.
   a. some people still complain about him   b. everyone works hard

   Although _____

4. Sam's teacher helped him a lot.
   a. Sam bought his teacher a gift   b. Sam decided to transfer to another class

   Even though _____

5. Jim doesn't like his job.
   a. he stays because of the salary   b. his boss is very critical

   Although _____

6. Peter got an A on the final exam.
   a. he decided to drop the class   b. the accounting class was very hard

   _____ even though _____

B **Talk** with a partner. Compare Ms. Muse with Mr. Grimes. Use *although* or *even though* and the cues provided.

Although Ms. Muse has a stressful job, she always has a smile on her face.

Although Mr. Grimes has an easy job, he never smiles at anybody.

1. has a stressful job /
   always has a smile on her face

2. always helps other people /
   has too much work

3. has a low salary /
   doesn't complain

4. is never late /
   lives far away

5. has a sick mother /
   never misses a day of work

6. has an easy job /
   never smiles at anybody

7. never helps others /
   has lots of time

8. has a good salary /
   says it's not enough

9. is often late /
   lives near the office

10. has no family responsibilities /
    is often absent from work

Write sentences about Ms. Muse and Mr. Grimes. Use *although* or *even though*.

Although Ms. Muse has a stressful job, she always has a smile on her face.
Ms. Muse always has a smile on her face although she has a stressful job.

3 Communicate

A **Work** in a small group. Choose one or more statements, and complete them with information about your life.

1. Our teacher is usually cheerful although . . .
2. Although I am happy to be in this country, . . .
3. _____ lost his/her job even though . . .
4. I have a good attitude at work/school even though . . .
5. Although I've only been in the United States for a short time, . . .

B **Share** information about your classmates.

Reading

1 Before you read

Talk with your classmates. Answer the questions.

1. When you are sick, what do you do to try to recover as quickly as possible?
2. How can having a positive attitude help someone who is sick?

2 Read

Read the story.

To listen to a recording of the reading, go to www.cambridge.org/transitions

The Power of Positive Thinking

HUGO ABITBOL came to the United States from Morocco 12 years ago. He went to college, found a job, got married, and had a son. His life was happy and normal in every way – until one day five years ago, when his idyllic world was turned upside down.

On that day, Hugo learned he had invasive prostate cancer. Although he was still a young man, he needed immediate surgery to save his life. He had the operation and spent two months recovering. Now, five years later, he is working and enjoying life as much as ever, even though he knows that the cancer could return any time.

"When life gives you a setback, you can't surrender. You can't give up. You have to persevere, although it's not always easy to keep going," Hugo said.

Hugo is sure it was his positive attitude that helped him overcome the cancer. It wasn't easy. At first, his family was stunned and upset. Hugo told them that they would deal with the challenges of his illness one day at a time.

"You can't stop living just because you have problems," Hugo said. "Even though life can be discouraging, you need to keep moving forward."

Following his surgery, Hugo took several positive steps to speed up his recovery. He joined a support group for cancer survivors. Connecting with other people reminded him that he was not alone and helped him deal with his anxiety about the future.

Also, he was determined to get back to his job managing a garden supply business. Hugo had always adored plants, and he enjoyed interacting with the customers. Having a job he loved helped him stay focused throughout his recovery.

Today, in addition to his job, Hugo volunteers with charities around Miami to help raise awareness about cancer. "I believe if you have the right attitude," he said, "positive things will happen. I count my blessings every day. I know I'm lucky to be here."

3 After you read

A Check your understanding.

1. What illness did Hugo have?
2. What did he do to overcome it?
3. What is Hugo doing today?

B Build your vocabulary.

1. Look for the words and phrases from the chart in the reading and underline them. Decide if the words are positive or negative. Fill in the clues that helped you guess.

Word	Positive	Negative	Clues
1. idyllic	✓		*happy, normal*
2. invasive			
3. setback			
4. persevere			
5. stunned			
6. anxiety			
7. determined			
8. adored			
9. focused			
10. count one's blessings			

2. Work with your classmates. Write four more words or phrases from the story that have a positive or negative meaning. Write *P* next to positive words. Write *N* next to negative words.

a. _____

b. _____

c. _____

d. _____

C Summarize the reading. Work with a partner and take turns restating the main points. Try to use vocabulary from Exercise B. Include the following:

1. Hugo's life before his illness
2. his operation
3. the steps in his recovery
4. the role of positive thinking
5. Hugo's life today

1 Before you read

Talk with your classmates. Answer the questions.

1. Read the title. What does the suffix *-itis* mean? Can you guess the meaning of *negativitis*?

2. Have you ever worked or studied with a negative person? How did this person's attitude affect you?

2 Read

Read the article.

To listen to a recording of the reading, go to www.cambridge.org/transitions

Say No to Negativitis

Meet Nelly. Even though she is healthy, does well in her night-school classes, and has a good job, Nelly finds something to complain about in almost every situation. It's a beautiful spring day? "All those flowers make me sneeze." She gets an A minus on a difficult homework assignment? "I should have gotten an A." She gets a pay increase at work? "It's only $20 a week. Big deal."

We all know people like Nelly. Critical, unsmiling, and gloomy, such people seem to have a disease that prevents them from seeing the bright side of life. Some psychologists even have a name for their negative attitude – "negativitis."

The causes of negativitis can be complex. Some people have a negative attitude because of difficulties in their childhood or personal lives. In other people, negativity is a response to unfair treatment. At work, for example, negativitis can develop from employees feeling that they are underpaid or overworked, that their successes are not recognized, or that they are not included in decision making.

Just one person's negative attitude can be enough to contaminate the atmosphere of an entire office or group. Workplaces infected with negativitis show increases in absenteeism, accidents, employee mistakes, and theft. Unless managers recognize employee negativity and take steps to eradicate it, it can lead to major financial losses.

Although management should take an active role in solving the problem of workplace negativity, you, as an employee, can also take steps to combat the toxic effects of negativitis in your workplace or group:

1. Whenever possible, avoid negative, complaining co-workers.

2. Control your own negative comments and negative thinking. *Choose* to think and speak positively.

3. Don't participate in office gossip.

4. Make a list of all the negative words you hear other people using. Remove those words from your vocabulary.

5. Notice and acknowledge other people's good work. Be generous with compliments.

6. Keep the lines of communication open with your boss and co-workers. Seek positive solutions to problems.

3 After you read

A **Check** your understanding.

1. The writer uses the words *contaminate*, *infect*, and *toxic* to compare a negative attitude to what?
2. What are some causes of negativitis?
3. What are the consequences of negativitis in the workplace?
4. Name three things that employees can do to combat negativitis at work.
5. Do you think negativitis is really a disease? Why or why not?

B **Build** your vocabulary.

1. Look for the words in the reading that end with the suffixes in the chart and underline them. Fill in each word's part of speech and its meaning. If necessary, use a dictionary to check your answers.

Suffix	Example in reading	Part of speech	Meaning
1. -itis	*negativitis*	*noun*	*illness of negative thinking*
2. -ity			
3. -ist			
4. -ism			
5. -hood			
6. -ate			

2. Work with a partner. Make a list of other words you know that end with the suffixes in the chart. Share your list with your classmates.

_____ _____ _____

_____ _____ _____

C **Summarize** the reading. Close your books. Work with a partner and take turns restating the main points. Then work with a partner to write the summary. Try to use the words in Exercise B. Include the following:

1. definition of negativitis
2. characteristics of negative people
3. causes and effects of negativitis
4. the role of management
5. what employees can do

Writing

1 Before you write

A Talk with a partner. Answer the questions.

1. In the United States, students are usually required to write an essay as part of a college application. What kinds of questions do you think students have to answer for such an essay?
2. Have you ever read or written a college admissions essay? If so, what was it about?

B Read Jane's college admissions essay to the University of South Florida. Underline all the positive statements she makes about herself and the school.

University of South Florida – Application (continued)
_____

Question: Please tell us about yourself and your career goals for the future. Why would you like to attend the University of South Florida?

    I am a senior at West Palms High School in Tampa, Florida. In May I will graduate from my high school with honors, and from there I plan to pursue my lifelong dream of becoming a marine biologist.

    I have lived in Florida all my life and have been interested in marine life since I was a child. I attended summer camps with a focus on marine biology and enjoyed every aspect of learning about ocean life. Although I am interested in both plants and animals, I would like to focus on studying animal life in the ocean.

    In preparation for college, I took every biology course offered by my high school, including two advanced marine biology courses in my junior and senior years. I got A's in all my science courses and I am finishing high school with an overall GPA of 3.9.

    The University of South Florida is the perfect school for me because of its excellent program in marine biology. I looked over your course catalog and was impressed by the diverse class offerings you have in this department. The reputation of the program is well-known. Additionally, your location close to the Gulf of Mexico is ideal for studying marine life. Finally, I am especially looking forward to taking classes with Dr. Kelly Spires, who wrote the textbooks for my marine biology classes in high school.

    For all of these reasons, I am very interested in attending the University of South Florida. Because of my strong interest in marine biology and the work I have already done in this area, I believe that I am a strong candidate for your program.

C Plan your answer to the same college admissions essay question that Jane answered. Take notes in the chart.

Name of the college or university you would like to attend: _____

Questions	Your notes
Paragraph 1: Your background and goals • Where you are from? • Where did you attend high school? • What are your interests? • What would you like to study? • What career would you like to have in the future? Why?	
Paragraph 2: Your preparation • What have you already done (courses, programs, travel, jobs) to prepare for your goal or career?	
Paragraph 3: Reasons for choosing this school	
Paragraph 4: Closing statement • Repeat your interest in the school • Make a positive closing statement about yourself	

2 Write

Write an answer to the question. Use Exercises 1B and 1C to help you.

3 After you write

A Check your writing.

	Yes	No
1. I wrote about my background.	☐	☐
2. I wrote about my career goals for the future.	☐	☐
3. I explained why I want to attend this college or university.	☐	☐
4. I ended with a positive statement about myself.	☐	☐

B Share your writing with a partner.

1. Take turns. Read your writing to a partner.
2. Comment on your partner's writing. Ask your partner questions. Tell your partner one thing you learned.

Get ready

1 Talk about the pictures

A What kinds of things do people write at work? At school?

B What do you think the people in the photos are typing or writing? Why do you think so?

Writing at work and school

2 Listening

A 🔘 **Listen** and answer the questions.

1. Why are writing skills important, according to the lecture?

2. What are some of the findings in the report of the National Commission on Writing for America's Families, Schools, and Colleges?

3. What can you do to improve your writing, according to the lecture?

B 🔘 **Listen again.** Take notes on the key information.

Introduction

   Topic:

   Examples:

Importance of writing

(findings from the report of the National Commission on Writing for

America's Families, Schools, and Colleges)

   1.

   2.

   3.

   4.

Report's conclusions

   1.

   2.

How to improve your writing:

Listen again. Check your answers. Did you miss anything important?

C Discuss. Talk with your classmates.

1. According to the lecture, writing should be clear, accurate, and concise. What do these words mean?

2. What types of writing do you need to do now? How might this change in the future?

3. Do you have a goal for improving your writing skills? If so, how do you plan to achieve it?

Causative verbs

1 Grammar focus: *Make*, *Have*, and *Get*

The causative verbs *make*, *have*, and *get* can mean that one person forces, asks, or persuades another person to do something. In causative sentences, the second verb does not change in tense or number.

Example	Form	Meaning
Mrs. Ovid made her son mow the lawn and walk the dog.	*make* + object + verb	Mrs. Ovid required him to do the chores. He had no choice.
Mrs. Ovid had a handyman fix the broken window.	*have* + object + verb	Mrs. Ovid asked (or paid) the handyman to do a service for her.
Mrs. Ovid got her neighbor to walk the dog while she was away.	*get* + object + *to* + verb	Mrs. Ovid persuaded her neighbor to do a favor for her.

2 Practice

A Write. Rewrite the sentences using *make*, *have*, or *get*.

1. Mrs. Ramsey asked her daughter to answer the phone.

   Mrs. Ramsey had her daughter answer the phone.

2. The boss required everyone to come in early.

   _____

3. Corina paid a manicurist to give her a manicure.

   _____

4. Ajay persuaded a classmate to proofread his history paper.

   _____

5. The school required all the parents to sign a consent form before the children's field trip.

   _____

6. Katarina persuaded all her friends to read her blog.

   _____

7. The school paid a gardener to plant flowers in front of the building.

   _____

8. The city asked a famous artist to paint a mural on the new bridge.

   _____

B **Talk** with a partner. Dr. Brown is the principal of Hamilton High School. Make sentences about her activities.

> Dr. Brown made a student stay after school.

Dr. Brown

make	have	get
1. a student / stay after school	4. the janitor / repair a broken window	7. some students / come to school on Saturday to paint over graffiti
2. teachers / come to an important meeting during their lunch hour	5. her assistant / water the plants in her office	8. the parents' association / raise money for a new gym floor
3. her assistant / retype a memo	6. some honor students / show visitors around the campus	9. the mayor / visit the school

Write sentences about Dr. Brown. Use *make*, *have*, or *get*.

Dr. Brown made a student stay after school.

3 Communicate

A **Take** notes on things that one person made, had, or got another person to do. Include your co-workers, classmates, friends, or family members in your notes.

Make	Have	Get
teacher / me / rewrite my essay	I / former boss / write me a letter of recommendation	My sister / me / babysit for her children

B **Work** with a partner. Make true sentences using your notes. Respond to your partner's sentences.

> *A* My teacher made me rewrite my essay
> *B* Why?
> *A* I made a lot of careless mistakes.

> *A* I had my former boss write me a letter of recommendation.
> *B* Did you have to wait a long time?
> *A* No, just a few days.

> *A* My sister got me to babysit for her children.
> *B* Did you mind?
> *A* No, she babysits for my children sometimes, too.

C **Share** information about your partner with the class.

Reading

1 Before you read

Talk with your classmates. Answer the questions.

1. What is *etiquette*? Give examples.
2. Do you think e-mail is a good way to communicate with friends and family? Why or why not?

2 Read

Read the article.

To listen to a recording of the reading, go to www.cambridge.org/transitions

E-mail Etiquette 101

The use of electronic communication has exploded throughout the world in the last decade. In the United States, recent studies have shown that 92 percent of all Internet users communicate via e-mail.

Innovative forms of electronic communication, such as text messaging and "tweeting" (sending short messages of less than 140 characters), are becoming more popular among teens and other computer-savvy people. However, most electronic communication at work and at school still revolves around e-mail messages.

Unfortunately, while many classes and seminars focus on correct ways to write a report or business letter, few, if any, stress the importance of using proper e-mail etiquette. To avoid miscommunication and angry responses, follow these rules:

Composing e-mail

Be sure to clearly say what the message is about in the subject line. If the subject in your subject line is too vague, your e-mail may not even be read.

With bosses, instructors, and new business contacts, keep e-mail formal until you are told that using first names is OK. Keep your e-mail brief and make the tone friendly and respectful. Remember to use good manners, like saying "please" and "thank you."

Don't type in all capital or in all lowercase letters. The first way may make it look like you are shouting, and the second may suggest that you are lazy.

Remember that e-mail messages are not private and that they can be seen by other people. Never fight or gossip in an e-mail message at work.

Sending and forwarding e-mail

Wait to enter the address until after you write the e-mail. That way, you will be more likely to complete the message before sending it. Take time to proofread both the message and the address. Refrain from using the "Reply all" feature unless you are sure everyone on the list needs to read it.

Responding to e-mail in a timely manner is essential. Even if you can't reply right away, send a response saying you received the message and will respond more fully later.

If you want to send a large attachment with an e-mail, ask first. If an attachment is too large, it may not be delivered. It may be best to break up a large attachment into a few smaller ones and to attach them to several different e-mails.

When it comes to forwarding e-mail, always add a comment to the forwarded message to tell why you are forwarding it and to identify yourself. And remember, do not send personal e-mail from your workplace.

3 After you read

A **Check** your understanding.

1. Name three rules to follow when composing an e-mail.
2. Name three rules to follow when sending an e-mail.
3. Why do you think proper e-mail etiquette is important? Can you think of any rules that the article left out? What are they?

B **Build** your vocabulary.

1. Look for the words from the chart in the reading and underline them.

2. Write a definition or synonym for each word. Then write an antonym, a word with the opposite meaning. Use a dictionary or thesaurus if necessary.

Word	Synonym	Antonym
1. innovative	*new, modern*	*old-fashioned*
2. savvy		
3. proper		
4. vague		
5. respectful		
6. private		
7. timely		

3. Work in a small group. Read the sentences with the words in the reading. Then use the antonyms to write related sentences with the opposite meaning. For example:

Sentence from the reading: "Innovative forms of electronic communication, such as text messaging and 'tweeting' . . . are becoming more popular . . ."

Your sentence: *These days, handwritten letters are an old-fashioned method of communication.*

C **Summarize** the reading. Work with a partner and take turns restating the main points. Then work together to write a summary. Try to use the vocabulary in Exercise B. Include the following topics:

1. importance of e-mail etiquette
2. etiquette for composing an e-mail
3. etiquette for sending and forwarding an e-mail

1 Before you read

Talk with your classmates. Answer the questions.

1. Look at the title of the reading. What do you think it means?
2. Do you think business writing differs from writing for school? How?

2 Read

Read the article.

To listen to a recording of the reading,
go to www.cambridge.org/transitions

Good Business Writing Doesn't Beat Around the Bush

The daily workplace is filled with writing of all sorts, lengths, and purposes, generated by both workers and management. E-mails, letters, memos, and reports are regularly distributed and read to keep information flowing smoothly.

The workplace is also filled with lots to read from the outside world. Newspapers, journals, news releases, and documents of all kinds are required reading for businesspeople who want to stay informed and on top of new developments.

But because time is short, businesspeople often just skim or only partially read things in order to extract the information they need. Therefore, it's key for business writing to be clear, crisp, and to the point.

All forms of effective writing in the workplace share several common qualities:

The K.I.S.S. Technique

First and foremost, good business writing uses the *K.I.S.S.* technique, meaning Keep It Short and Simple. The idea is to convey information in simple, well-organized, and easy-to-read terms. You can avoid confusion by using short sentences when possible and keeping the language simple and familiar. This aids the comprehension of readers who may not have time to read the material in depth.

Directness

Good business writing doesn't beat around the bush, but instead is direct, specific, and to the point. Fuzzy, abstract phrases, such as "a nice person" or "a good idea," force readers to slow down and guess at their real meaning. Concrete, descriptive phrases, such as "a generous young woman" or "an innovative suggestion," enable readers to form clearer images in their minds.

The Active Voice

The passive voice can sometimes confuse readers because it does not say who the performer of an action is. In business writing, it is especially important to be clear about exactly who is doing what.

Thus, instead of saying "Arrangements were made to ship your order immediately," you can write "I made arrangements to ship your order immediately." Instead of "Your complaint is being investigated," write "I am having my assistant investigate your complaint." The active voice not only tells the reader who is responsible for performing the action, it is also more interesting and attention grabbing.

3 After you read

A Check your understanding.

1. Why is it important to keep business writing short and simple?
2. What is the K.I.S.S. technique?
3. Name two ways that using the active voice can make writing more effective.

B Build your vocabulary.

1. Look for the words from the chart in the reading and underline them. Write the meaning from the article.

2. Use a dictionary and write a different meaning for each word.

Word	Meaning in article	Other meaning
1. on top of (prep.)	*informed about*	*at the highest point*
2. short (adj.)		
3. skim (v.)		
4. key (adj.)		
5. crisp (adj.)		
6. fuzzy (adj.)		
7. concrete (adj.)		

3. Work with a partner. Write sentences using the other meaning of the words in the chart.

We had another hiker take a picture of us on top of the mountain.

C Summarize the reading. Work with a partner and take turns restating the main points. Then work together to write a summary. Try to use the vocabulary from Exercise B. Include the following topics:

1. key characteristics of business writing
2. the K.I.S.S. technique
3. directness in writing
4. using the active voice

Writing

1 Before you write

A **Talk** with your classmates. Answer the questions.

1. What types of reports are written at work? Give examples.
2. Have you ever heard the term "action plan"? Can you guess the purpose of this kind of report?

B **Read** the action plan written by the Office of Student Affairs at a college.

CITY COLLEGE
Office of Student Affairs

Cell-phone Cheating

A growing problem on our campus is students' use of cell phones to cheat on exams. The number of students caught cheating this way increased by more than 15 percent in the past year. The cheating takes several forms:

1. Students send text messages with the answers to test questions to other students in the room.

2. Students photograph test items or test pages and send them to students outside the class.

This cheating has serious consequences for our college. First, students who do not cheat are forced to compete unfairly against those who do. Second, instructors who wish to prevent cheating must spend time and resources creating alternative versions of tests. Third, news about cheating on campus damages the reputation of the college in the community.

To prevent cell-phone cheating, the Office of Student Affairs recommends the following new procedures:

1. Upon entering the exam room, students carrying cell phones must turn them off and leave them with the exam proctor at the front of the room.

2. Students will not be allowed to carry backpacks or heavy jackets to their seats.

3. For classes of 25 or more students, the college will hire additional proctors to supervise exams.

4. Students caught cheating will receive an automatic score of zero on the exam, and they will be required to attend a disciplinary meeting with the Dean of Students.

A notice regarding these new regulations will appear in the college newspaper next Friday, April 20, and it will continue to appear twice a week for the next month. Implementation of the new procedures will begin during spring semester final exams, which will take place May 20–27.

C **Talk** with a partner. Identify and summarize the following parts of the action plan in the model:

1. the problem
2. the consequences of the problem
3. recommendations for solving the problem
4. a schedule for implementing the solutions

D **Plan** an action plan in response to a problem in your class, school, job, or personal life. Use the diagram to organize your writing. Share your diagram with a partner.

Problem: _____

Consequence(s)	Recommendation(s)	Schedule
1. _____	1. _____	Apr. 20: _____
2. _____	2. _____	Apr. 20–May 20: _____
3. _____	3. _____	May 20–27: _____
	4. _____	

2 Write

Write the action plan. Include the problem, consequence(s), recommendation(s), and time line. Use Exercises 1C and 1D to help you.

3 After you write

A **Check** your writing.

	Yes	No
1. The introductory paragraph introduces and describes the problem.	☐	☐
2. I made recommendations for solving the problem.	☐	☐
3. I suggested a time line for solving the problem.	☐	☐

B **Share** your writing with a partner.

1. Take turns. Read your action plan to a partner.
2. Comment on your partner's writing. Ask your partner questions. Tell your partner one thing you learned.

Photography credits

TRACK LISTING FOR SELF-STUDY AUDIO CD

Track	Page	Exercise	Track	Page	Exercise
1			7	53	2
2	3	2	8	63	2
3	13	2	9	73	2
4	23	2	10	83	2
5	33	2	11	93	2
6	43	2			